I0098282

DIVE-ABLED

The Leo Morales Story

DIVE-ABLED

The Leo Morales Story

ERIC DOUGLAS

WITH

LEO MORALES

BEST PUBLISHING COMPANY

Copyright © 2017 Best Publishing Company

All photos provided provided by the authors except when noted specifically. Permission granted to publisher for quotes from individuals in the book.

ISBN: 978-1-947239-02-9 (print)
978-1-947239-03-6 (ebook)

Library of Congress Number: 2017956026

All rights reserved. No part of this book may be reproduced, stored in a retrieval system, or transmitted in any form or by any means electronic, mechanical, photocopying, microfilming, recording, or otherwise without permission from the publisher.

Best Publishing Company
631 US Highway 1, Suite 307
North Palm Beach, FL 33408

The opinions expressed in this work are those of the authors and do not reflect the opinions of Best Publishing Company or its editors.

Information contained in this work has been obtained by BPC and the authors from sources believed to be reliable. Neither BPC nor its authors guarantees the accuracy of completeness of any information published herein, and neither BPC nor its authors shall be responsible for any errors, omissions, or claims for damages, including exemplary damages, arising out of use, inability to use, or with regard to the accuracy or sufficiency of the information contained in this publication.

Diving is an activity that has inherent risks. An individual may experience injury resulting in disability or death. All person who wish to engage in diving activities must receive professional instruction. The authors, publisher, and any other party associated with production of this book does not accept responsibility for any accident or injury resulting from diving.

Front Cover Courtesy of Lynton Francois Burger

Dedication

This book is dedicated to my ladies: Beverly, Kaitlin, Ashlin and Jamison. Thank you all for accepting the long hours in front of the computer that comes with being a writer. Your patience allows me to tell stories, like this one, that I hope inspires others for years to come.

Eric Douglas

I dedicate this book to:

- my beloved wife Larena, who always gave me the courage to go on in the midst of adversity and made me feel that dreams are achievable if you have faith and the heart to fight for them;

- my father for the valuable lessons he taught me throughout his life;

- my mother who instilled in me the values that did not let me surrender;

- my brothers Ricardo and Araceli, who have been at my side with their wholehearted support every step of the way; and

- God for giving me the opportunity to write a new story where I can be the best version of myself.

Leo Morales

Foreword

After returning from military service with the United States Navy in 1969, I attended Wright State University (WSU) in Dayton, Ohio. WSU was noted for making education accessible to anyone with a desire to learn despite any physical limitations. Its desire to successfully mainstream students regardless of ability attracted students from all over the world.

While completing my bachelor's degree in biology, I approached the university's Health, Physical Education and Recreation (HPR) Department about creating a comprehensive diver education program at WSU. The WSU Scuba Program soon became one of the country's premiere, college-level diver education programs.

Once the first diver education/certification courses were offered, it wasn't surprising to see students with disabilities wanting to become certified divers. Since, in those early years, there were no accepted standards available to assist scuba instructors in modifying skills to accommodate divers with physical limitations, diving educators had to be very creative to adapt training standards designed for divers without limitations.

Although there were certainly challenges for a student with a disability, it was no less challenging for the instructor. I adapted what I had learned in the military: when confronted with a problem, fully analyze it, adapt your approach, and overcome the limitation. This approach allowed us to successfully introduce scuba diving to many who were otherwise denied access to this wonderful sport. Not because they were not capable but because the sport, at the time, was unable to accommodate them.

Luckily, this situation changed with the advent of numerous organizations that have developed comprehensive standards for all levels of diver education while becoming staunch advocates for divers regardless of limitations. One of the continuing challenges with encouraging people with physical limitations to learn to scuba dive has been the limited number of positive role models in our sport. This is where Leo Morales has had his greatest impact.

While attending an annual Diving Equipment and Marketing Association (DEMA) trade show, I had the pleasure of meeting a person who has brought a new and exciting dimension to the term "role model." That man was Leo Morales. What immediately caught my eye was his broad smile and his excited gestures to a bevy of diving professionals who seemed to be mesmerized by his energy. Creating that kind of enthusiasm has attracted scores of others to him and certainly attracted me.

I said to myself, "I have to get to know this man." As I moved closer, it was only then I noticed his crutches. He had lost his right leg to cancer.

Cancer is a terrible disease and overcoming the physical as well as the psychological damage it creates is no easy feat. As a cancer survivor myself, I felt I was in the presence of a man who could virtually overcome any obstacle. The potentially devastating effects of the loss of a limb from his disease seemed to have inspired rather than defeated him.

His infectious smile and boundless enthusiasm are only a few of the traits that make Leo Morales a standout personality in our sport and industry. As he will tell you, "Scuba diving saved my life." Well, the saving of his life has certainly enriched the lives of countless others who, because of him, have come to realize scuba diving is a truly inclusive sport where a person is judged by abilities not limitations.

Through his desire to share the experience with everyone regardless of limitation, Leo has transformed lives by opening the doorway to a world below the surface of the water filled with wonders and excitement not found anywhere else on earth. Leo's story is both inspirational and motivational. Our sport and our lives are better because of him.

Enjoy the read and let Leo's story inspire you to achieve your dreams!

Dan Orr, President Dan Orr Consulting LLC
Member, Hall of Fame for Divers with Disabilities
Member, International Scuba Diving Halls of Fame
Recipient, DEMA Reaching Out Award
Member, NAUI Hall of Honor
President, Academy of Underwater Arts and Sciences
Chairman, WCH Media Group Board of Directors
President Emeritus, Divers Alert Network (DAN)

Preface

first met Leo in December 2013, the day before he was scheduled to complete his second world-record dive across the Cozumel Marine Park, and was immediately struck by the presence of the man. The first thing you notice is his shoulders and chest, not his missing leg. He is a big, strong man. You next notice his infectious smile and thick, dark hair. Some of Leo's most memorable traits are his energy and the ever-present thumbs-up he uses to signal agreement and encouragement. It's only after you step back and look him up and down that you see the crutches tucked up underneath his bulky biceps. From there, your eyes wander down to the missing leg.

On that first day we met, I was so struck by him that I felt compelled to immediately share his story with my readers. The next day, after he successfully completed the dive, I posted a column on my website about this incredible person who had just completed something miraculous. At the time, I wrote:

"While his records may have the phrase 'with a disability' attached to them, it certainly doesn't lessen the accomplishments. The mental focus necessary to accomplish something like that is phenomenal. He had to maintain his Nautilus rebreather, continually swim, stay warm and alert, and concentrate on what he was doing for more than eight hours.

"Most divers will never attempt anything like Leo's dives. The lesson I take from watching Leo and enjoying his warm, inviting, and positive outlook is, 'Nothing is impossible.' You can't let anything stand in your way. In interviews, he has described the days after the cancer and the surgery to remove his leg as the darkest days of his life and a time in which he considered taking his own life. The surgery saved his life but he only had an estimated twenty percent chance of surviving.

"With the support of his friends, family, and God, he returned to diving and now works as an advocate for the disabled in his native Mexico. His dives aren't stunts; they are designed to inspire everyone and also to show people with disabilities that they can do anything they set their minds to.

"Most of us will never have to face anything as terrible as a surgery to save our lives that may kill us in the process. Most of us will never have to lose a large portion of our bodies to disease. Yet, too many of us use the words 'I can't' on a too-regular basis. Meeting Leo has definitely inspired me; the inspiration isn't about diving at all. It is about life.

From now on, every time I say 'I can't,' I'm going to ask myself why. Would Leo say I can't? And then I will get up and do it, regardless of what anyone else says."

Flash-forward about a year, and Leo and I agreed to work together on this book. I live in West Virginia and Leo is in Mexico, but we decided to conduct a number of interviews through Skype. I recorded them as we discussed life, the dives, and his plans for the future. I tried to capture his strength, his will, and his enthusiasm. He never stops moving, never stops struggling, and never stops working toward his goal.

As you read this book and learn more about Leo, I believe you will feel the same inspiration that I have.

Eric Douglas
Pinch, West Virginia
2017

Chapter 1

"Scuba diving saved my life."

You will often hear people make broad statements without having faced true adversity. They've never wanted to end it all because of something that happened in their lives. They've never had to fight to walk again or felt like they were less of a person than they were before. And they never found joy, peace, inspiration and purpose in something.

But Leo Morales has.

By his own admission, Leo "had it all." He was an up-and-coming young professional who had fun and made money. At twenty-eight years old, he became a bank director and won several awards for performance. His star rose fast and he enjoyed the ride.

Until 2008.

He felt a strange pain in his lower back. He wrote it off to sitting at his desk as he worked long hours at the bank. Finally, he gave in and consulted a doctor. The news was shocking. He had cancer. The tumor was on the inside of his right leg and right buttock. It weighed three kilos (6.6 pounds). The doctors told him there was a serious risk the cancer could spread into his vital organs. The only solution? Remove his entire right leg. The odds were high he would not survive the surgery. If he did, the doctors said he would have a five-year life expectancy.

Leo describes the decision to have the surgery as a leap of faith. There was a good chance he would never wake up from the anesthesia. There was a good chance he would never leave the hospital. He said goodbye to everyone he knew and loved and went to sleep on the operating table asking God for "one more day of life."

———

Leo's life began on March 26, 1973. The oldest of three children born to Leobardo Morales Santos and Araceli Cervantes Carrillo, he lived with his parents in Mexico City through elementary school with his younger sister, Araceli, and younger brother, Ricardo. An earthquake hit when he was twelve years old.

Leo described the time as "terrible, with dead bodies in the streets and buildings falling down."

His father picked him up from school just before the building collapsed, killing some of his classmates. The destruction upset his mother so badly she convinced Leo's father, a singer, to move the family to Merida, a proud city on Mexico's Yucatan Peninsula. She was a native Yucateco, and the family had a second house there. Leo's father didn't adapt well, and the move caused some strain in Leo's parents' marriage.

When Leo finished middle school, Leo's father decided to move the family back to Mexico City. Although a crowded city, it had opportunities for a singer. The family was put under further strain when his parents were in a serious car accident. Leo's mother spent most of the next year in bed recovering from her injuries. Leo stepped up and helped his family, caring for his parents as they recovered. The strain resulting from the accident drove a greater wedge into the family unit and eventually his parents divorced. Leo went back and forth between his parents, but when it came time to go to the university, he decided to stay with his mother to help her out with his siblings.

Living in the Yucatan with his mother was a challenge for Leo. She was very conservative and scared of everything.

He said, "She was always saying, 'Don't do this and don't do that.'"

Leo describes his own behavior at this point in his life as "aggressive." He was angry at the world because of the situation with his family and their accident. He worked as a waiter in a restaurant and studied tourism. When he turned nineteen, Leo's parents sent him back to Merida to get him away from Mexico City, concerned about the trouble he was getting into.

"I was a typical troublemaker guy."

They wanted him out of the capital city and close to his mother's family. In August 1992, he met Larena Loria and everything changed.

"I got her hand and I never let go. A woman can change your life forever."

Over the next two years, Leo worked as a security guard in the best disco club in town, Tequila Rocks.

"That was very cool," he said.

Even then, Leo was notable for his broad shoulders and strong arms. As he got older, he knew he wanted more out of life and as his relationship with Larena grew, he decided it was time to return to school. In 1994, he entered the Merida Institute of Technology, studying for a career in business administration and marketing. He joined the student council of the alumni association. When he graduated in 1996, he had a reputation for being well-liked among his peers.

After finishing up at the university, he took a job as an account officer at a bank branch in Cancun. Two years later, in 1998, he left to work with another company and was transferred to a bank in Quintana Roo as an account executive. He stayed there until 2000 when another bank hired him as a branch manager.

The next few years flew by for Leo and Larena. They were married on September 18, 1999, in front of a small group of friends in Merida. Leo worked at the bank and Larena taught at a local school. They were happy and enjoying their lives.

On February 12, 2004, Leo had a motorcycle accident on his way to work and broke his right leg. The doctors in Cancun weren't up to the task of saving his leg, so he was transferred to Mexico City for what eventually took seven surgeries, one of which lasted more than twelve hours. In all, he spent five months in the hospital in Mexico City before returning home in July 2004.

In spite of the care he got in Mexico City, Leo struggled. He was in pain, and his leg wasn't healing correctly. Through a friend with contacts in Cuba, Leo went to Havana to meet with the orthopedic doctor who cared for Cuban President Fidel Castro when the leader fell and broke his hip. Leo wanted a second opinion about his options for healing.

Entering the National Hotel in Havana, Leo slipped and fell. The cleaning staff was polishing the floor, but no one had bothered to put out a sign to warn tourists. When he fell on the hard marble floor, Leo broke his right leg again.

"It was an awful experience. They told me to get up and move to my room. Because I was a tourist, they told me the treatment would cost no less than 100,000 euros. All they wanted was to take my money."

Leo was lying on the floor of the hotel lobby in pain and no one was able to help him. No one could give him any painkillers unless he went to the hospital. The friend who brought Leo to Cuba started making phone calls. Leo called his health insurance company in Mexico. They told him he was covered, but they couldn't care for him in Cuba. He would need to get home.

"I was finally able to get up in spite of the pain, paid my bill, and left. They got me to the airport. My friend went to the immigration counter with my passport. They said if your friend cannot walk and come to the cameras, he cannot fly."

He hobbled to the immigration counters to get his passport stamped and leave Cuba. Leo's friend bribed someone, and they got an ambulance to the airplane. Two men carried him up the steps to the airplane. Seated on the plane, Leo's ordeal wasn't over yet.

"The soldiers came on the plane. They said I was a Cuban guy escaping. The flight attendant asked me what was going on. The Cuban military people were threatening everyone. I was crying and in pain. The pilot finally told the Cuban military to get off the plane. He said it was a Mexican plane, and so it was Mexican territory."

They finally left Cuba and Leo returned to Mexico City with a broken leg.

———

In January 2005, Leo was physically able to return to his job. He was now a bank director, the youngest person in the region to have that position. Everything indicated he had a prosperous and bright future ahead of him. Things went well for Leo and Larena for the next three years. They continued to enjoy life and be in love.

In February 2008, he began to experience pain in his right buttock and hip. He tolerated the pain for a while, convincing himself it was pain related to his earlier injures. Larena eventually convinced him to go to the hospital. The doctor's first instincts agreed with Leo's own opinion. They said because of his earlier problems and because he was a big man, he was likely having problems with his sciatic nerve. His back pain was lower back pain without a specific cause but the doctor ordered an X-ray anyway. He then saw shadows that weren't natural.

At this point, they didn't know what they were dealing with, but Leo and Larena knew it was serious.

In April, Leo flew back to Mexico City where the doctors performed a biopsy and discovered Leo had a cancerous tumor weighing more than three kilos (six pounds). His diagnosis was an aggressive form of cancer, chondrosarcoma. It was stage three or four. The doctors agreed the best treatment was forty radiation sessions without chemotherapy.

At the end of the sessions, the doctors came back to him with bad news. The radiation hadn't worked and the tumor was still growing. They gave him a life expectancy of three or four months. The doctors at the Mexico City hospital told him the only way to save his life was a complete leg amputation, all the way to his hip. Because of the weakened state of his immune system following the radiation therapy, they only gave him a twenty percent chance of living through the surgery. Out of options and not ready to give up, Leo and Larena opted for the surgery. Twenty percent chance of survival was better than a death sentence.

On September 25, 2008, Leo entered the hospital for a hip disarticulation surgery.

"My parents were there. That's when I realized just how serious this was. Everyone said their goodbyes. I thought I would never wake up. Other people with cancer and leukemia told me that I was lucky because I still had hope, but I didn't feel like I was lucky at the time," he said. "I wasn't a religious person, but by the time I went into the surgery room, I prayed to God for help."

The surgery took eight hours. One of the first things he noticed when he woke up in intensive care was absence. He looked down and saw flat white bed sheets on the hospital bed where his leg had once been, where it was supposed to be. He was alive but physically incomplete.

"I took a deep breath and looked around. I was completely on pain drugs so I raised my head. I was covered with a sheet and saw my one foot and then an empty space where my right foot should be. I said 'Okay,' and thanked God that I was still alive."

Leo spent the next two months in intensive care because the doctors were worried about the possibility of an infection. He also went through another thirty radiation treatments to remove all traces of tumor activity from his body.

Chapter 2

What came next was Leo's low point, a period he is still ashamed of. Coming home from the hospital after the surgery in December 2008, he struggled with his new reality.

"I was going to a psychiatrist and I felt like I was taking thirty pills a day, but I wasn't getting any better. I was just focused on my own misery. I had no sex drive because of the antidepressants I was taking," he said.

Leo finally reached rock bottom in the winter of 2009 and took all of his pills one night. They called his doctor to his home. Leo wouldn't wake up for two days, but they pulled him through it.

"I am really embarrassed by what I did. I was a coward. My wife really suffered during that period, but I was only worried about myself."

Around his birthday at the end of March 2009, Leo decided to take charge of his life and quit all of the medications they were giving him.

"I suffered like an addict, but I was able to get clean."

Since then, he hasn't taken any antidepressants. He has struggled with ongoing depression and other problems, but he won't go back to the medications.

In 2015, Larena finally reached her own breaking point from the pressure of caring for him. She began counseling and convinced him to return to therapy.

"They offered me medications again and I refused. The idea of taking those pills brings me nothing but bad memories."

———

There is no such thing as a "good" amputation, but the one Leo endured was one of the worst possible. At least when it comes to learning to walk and use a prosthesis. Most leg amputees have a hip joint that stabilizes the body in the device. In Leo's case, missing his entire leg, including the hip, he faced an even bigger challenge before he got out of bed. His doctors in Mexico told him he was never going to walk again.

"The doctors were not sure they were able to remove all the cancer," remembers Leo. "All I could think about was how much I wanted to live and all I had to live for."

In six months, a body scan would be done to see if the cancer was successfully removed. Unable to control the outcome, he chose to concentrate on his rehabilitation. He wanted to walk again. At thirty-six years old, he had to learn how to walk and use the toilet again. He faced physical therapy and endless visits with psychologists and psychiatrists to overcome the loss of a limb.

He quickly discovered there were no state-of-the-art prosthetic facilities in Mexico, and most amputees in his country were not mobile.

"Those who had lost limbs were not active and did not function well in society," he said.

Even after he had recovered physically from the surgery and the cancer treatments, by December 2008, Leo was depressed. He was drowning—not in the sea but in self-pity. He felt as though he was no longer a complete man and a burden to Larena. He had to relearn just about everything. The situation in Mexico made it worse. He felt like an outcast when people stared and pointed at him.

"The discrimination was awful. Everyone looked and pointed at me. I got really depressed. I was pushing my wife away. I told her she needed to find someone who could hold her hand. I couldn't do that anymore because I was using crutches. I thought I was a monster. That is the worst part of a disability. You need to accept it in your mind and love yourself. Most people can never do that," he explained about that dark time. "My wife was crying with me and saying, 'I love the way you are. When we got married, I promised that I would love you for good or bad or in sickness or in health.'"

Leo accepted an offer from a friend to get away and stay at a home in Orlando to relax. Leo and Larena headed for the United States. The trip became a turning point for Leo.

Understanding that attitudes toward disability and prosthetic services for men and women with missing legs had progressed further in the United States than at home, Leo and Larena made a list of places in the Orlando area where they could get Leo a prosthetic leg. They visited eight different clinics. Each one said they could make him a leg, but the leg would cost at least $50,000, and they wanted fifty percent of the money in advance—money Leo didn't have.

"I told my wife I was not going to be able to walk again, so let's forget about it."

They had one more place on the list, but Leo told Larena he didn't want to go.

"My wife said, 'We are here so what do we have to lose?' When I walked through the door, I knew it was going to be different."

Prosthetic and Orthotic Associates of Central Florida (POA) was owned by the inventor and prosthetist, Stan Patterson. When Leo met Stan, he told him he was really depressed and doctors said he would never walk again.

"Stan told me, 'Let's do it. I will make you walk in three days.' I told him it was impossible and it was not going to happen. He said, 'I can do it.'"

"After meeting with Stan and the POA staff, we knew this was the right place," says Leo. "We felt a deep level of trust and faith that they could help me."

Leo was interested in working with Stan, but he was also concerned about the cost.

"I was a banker and knew everything costs money.

We were running out of money."

He told Larena they were going back to POA the next day to tell Stan they didn't have any money. When they told him, Stan said not to worry about it.

"The following day, I took my first steps and I cried like a baby. It was the first time I realized the blessing to have shoes. To look down and see two feet. I cannot tell you how powerful that day was for me. They taught me how to walk again."

Stan knew helping a person who has had a hip disarticulation to walk again comes with a tremendous set of challenges.

He explained, "Leo was fit with a custom NPS hip-disarticulate socket and within two days of his arrival, was walking, using only a cane for support. Because hip disarticulates are missing all three joints (ankle, knee, and hip) necessary for walking, they are limited in activity due to the tremendous amount of energy they must use to simply take a step. The fact that Leo was young, strong, and incredibly determined to walk again played a big part in his success.

"Within a few days of being fit with his first prosthesis, he began walking with a cane, which is an extremely rare occurrence because only one to two percent of amputations are hip disarticulate, and of those, only twenty-five percent use a prosthesis. Every socket system must be custom-made due to differences in areas to be fit, such as bony prominences and the amount and contour of the remaining tissue. Rather than surrounding the entire pelvic and hip area with a rigid (industry standard) 'bucket' design socket, POA fabricates a custom pant liner to which other components, including our patented vacuum device, are attached.

"The tension can be released by the touch of a button, allowing for increased comfort when sitting and then tightened to provide more support when ambulating. This system is what initially drew Leo to check out POA and ultimately choose our facility," Stan explained.

"Challenges vary based on overall health and fitness of wearer, level of amputation, fit of prosthesis, and type of components that are used and available. In the case of a hip disarticulate amputee, use of a microprocessor knee greatly increases the ability to ambulate successfully."

POA does a lot of work with war veterans and others who have lost limbs, so Leo was working alongside many people who were worse off than he was.

"I realized I had lost one leg, but I met people who had lost two legs or two legs and two arms. They inspired me, and I knew I needed to go back to Mexico and inspire people. Just because we have lost a leg or an arm, we are not waste. We are able to do things."

Stan Patterson told Leo to take his new leg home and come back in two days. He wanted Leo to use the leg in real life. Fitted with the prosthesis, Leo left POA.

"We went to the park, and I was walking with my wife."

In the evenings, Leo and Larena dined in restaurants and shopped at the Florida Mall. Leo continued working hard on his gait training at POA and soon the cane was discarded and his confidence renewed.

In spite of the joy he felt at being able to walk again, Leo had a problem.

"I told Stan I had no money to pay for the leg. I came back and said I couldn't take it. I didn't have the money. I was walking in a $50,000 device. Just my knee cost $20,000. It was all electronic."

And that is where Leo's world was turned upside down. It's also when and where he decided to dedicate his life to working for others. Stan explained he made good money from the military contracts so from time to time, he liked to do pro bono work. He told Leo if he got the money later and wanted to pay him, that's fine, but don't worry about it. He said he wanted to do it to help people.

"POA hands me a prosthesis to walk again. Stan Patterson made a wonderful prosthesis for me. I learned to walk and rehabbed with several veterans and other amputees. I learned that sometimes life is hard, but there is always someone who is going through something worse than me. Right then, I decided to support and motivate people to continue living a good life. I want people to appreciate what they have. It is too easy to take everything we have for granted."

Feeling grateful for all he had experienced and accomplished in such a short time, Leo wanted to make a difference in the lives of others.

"I want to provide inspiration for other amputees, particularly hip disarticulates, who think that walking is not possible. Everywhere I go in Mexico, I am proud to show my prosthesis and tell people about my experience.

I am so thankful for all I have received. I want to shout 'POA! POA! POA!' I want every amputee to know this quality of care is available."

Chapter 3

In 2010, back in Mexico, Leo faced discrimination that he thought he had left behind.

Since Leo had gone to work for a Mexican bank as soon as he had graduated, banking was what he knew how to do. Now, Social Security Administration declared he was fit and able to go back to work.

"After twenty-five days, they fired me because they said disabled people were not the kind of people they wanted to see in the bank. That made me really sad. That's how I fed my family. They fired me. When I asked why, they said it was because I was disabled, and I couldn't do my job."

It took him a while, but eventually he remembered the feeling he had in Florida, thanks to the people who gave him his prosthetic leg. He got moving.

"Finally, I realized I was lucky. I was still alive, and I had my wife."

He also faced the limitations of time for the first time. Young and full of life before the cancer, he had never worried much about the future. Once he left the hospital, his doctors told him there was a good chance the cancer had metastasized and spread all over his body. They told him he only had five years of life left.

"I realized I had already wasted one year of my remaining life. I only had four more years."

To keep himself fit, Leo began swimming for exercise.

"A really good friend told me that I needed to try scuba diving. I thought, 'Yeah, let's do it. That would be fun!'"

Except it wasn't.

"I sank right to the bottom. It was awful. I couldn't move in the water. My weight belt was slipping off, and I didn't know how to handle it. My friends who were with me stayed next to me. After twenty minutes in the water, crying in my mask, I surfaced. I said 'I will never do this again.' They told me I just had to learn how to handle it. And I said, 'I'm not doing this again.'"

Leo's friends threatened to kidnap him and take him the next time they went diving, but fortunately that never had to happen. Leo's friend William Lotz encouraged him to try diving again. After a few weeks, he agreed to go. This time, things clicked. It took him a few moments to adapt to the situation, but then he began to control his buoyancy. He got comfortable in the warm, clear water near his home in Playa del Carmen, Mexico, and began to relax. Suddenly, he was in a new world. He could float weightless in the water and the loss of his leg was no longer a problem. He didn't feel the weight of the world.

"I had to learn how to move myself with my hands and establish my buoyancy. It was like being a baby and learning to walk," he explained. "I dived like forty minutes. When I surfaced, I said, 'I need to do this again.' I was free. I was free from my crutches. I was free from my wheelchair. I wasn't a disabled person in the water. That is the magic of scuba diving. It was one of the most wonderful experiences in my life. I cried again, but this time it was tears of happiness. For the first time, I found a place where I was able to do something really good."

Leo pursued diving. He had a purpose again and sought more training and experience. People with disabilities have been scuba diving since the early days of the sport, but only in recent years has it moved into more mainstream acceptance. There are a number of diving programs set up specifically for disabled veterans and people who have to use a wheelchair for mobility. In the water, they become weightless and regain freedom of movement that many thought they had lost forever.

Some people with disabilities earn traditional scuba diving certifications, meeting all of the requirements and performing all the same skills that any other diver would handle. They learn to swim through the water, perform self-rescue skills, and control their buoyancy in the water column simply by adapting their techniques.

In the case of a leg amputee, for example, a diver will kick with his remaining leg while adding in additional propulsion with his hands, often wearing webbed gloves.

Divers who are unable to perform the traditional skills with adaptations often seek scuba diving certifications from training agencies specifically set up to work with divers with disabilities. Often these divers are required to dive with one or two specially trained dive buddies who are prepared to propel them through the water or handle basic tasks like ear or mask clearing.

Once he learned how to adapt himself, his body and his technique, Leo was able to earn traditional dive certifications. On his first dive experience, after his amputation, he had trouble keeping his weight belt in place. His hip disarticulation amputation changed his hip structure, taking away the place his weight belt would normally rest. He had to relocate his weights to his BCD (buoyancy control device) to keep them in place.

A BCD is a device in the form of a jacket that holds the tank and regulator (breathing apparatus) in place. A diver can add air to an internal bladder in the BCD directly from the tank to float effortlessly in the water

Once he worked out those details, Leo was hooked on diving. "After that, I formally began my training in diving for no other reason than to prove to myself that I was moving forward. I took my last check from the bank and started dive training to just forget about it. I just wanted to dive to forget the real world."

He quickly earned his open water and advanced open water diver certifications and then moved on to pursuing and achieving professional ratings. "The day I became a divemaster was the happiest day of my life."

"Everything was to PADI and TDI standards. I didn't know any of the disabled diver standards existed. I moved forward using the regular standards."

PADI is the Professional Association of Diving Instructors and the world's largest scuba diving training agency. TDI (Technical Diving International) is the largest technical diving certification agency in the world. To keep him challenged, a friend suggested that Leo should move beyond recreational diving to technical diving. Technical diving involves greater depths, different breathing gases and equipment, and more risk. Most technical divers will say the appeal of technical diving isn't the risk, however. It is the mental and physical challenge of taking the human body to new levels.

"I was going to work with my friend Alessandra Figari, but she was busy and her father was sick, so I found German Yañez, a Mexican technical diving instructor. We talked about the course. At the end of the conversation, I told him, "I don't know if you know me, but I am missing my right leg."

Leo continued. "There are a lot of really good people in the diving community. They have been incredibly supportive of me. I started doing my technical courses, decompression procedures, attend a trimix class, and then I became a trimix diver."

Trimix is a mixture of three noble gases: oxygen, nitrogen, and helium. They are blended together in proportions specific to the depth of the dive. The percentages of each gas are fine-tuned in the tank to lower the risk of narcosis and decompression sickness.

Technical diving training involves a lot of study and classroom work, but it also takes a lot of diving and experience in the water.

Diving was taking the place of physical therapy and keeping Leo active. But it was doing something even more important. It was giving him a purpose and a goal to work toward. In the beginning, he was just doing it for himself. But that was soon to change.

"I began the training, but it's not just about the training. You have to go out and dive regularly to be proficient. It takes regular practice. One day I was diving with four or five tanks at the same time, but recreational divers were on the boat, and they looked at me preparing for the technical dive. They said I was inspirational. I was diving that way to conquer my own limitations. I was trying to prove to myself I had the same capabilities as a regular person. I didn't feel like a superman. I was doing it just for me."

The idea of inspiring others was the furthest thing from Leo's mind at that point. But those fellow divers planted a seed in his mind.

"When people told me I was inspirational, I said, 'You know what? I can do something really good.' People told me I needed to share this with the world."

He wasn't sure how to go about it, but he liked the idea that he could serve as an inspiration for others, just like he had been encouraged and inspired at Prosthetics and Orthotics Associates.

"One day I was talking with my instructor about doing something with scuba diving that would make a statement and encourage others. I told German this is a really good opportunity to prove disability is a matter of perception. I said, 'Let's do something.' I searched on the Internet, and there were very few people who did technical diving as a disabled diver. I said to my friends one day that I needed to send a message and they all said, 'We are with you.' We didn't have any money or experience in this. None of us had a dime, not a clue how to do it, but we started working to make it happen."

And this is where the story of Leo really begins. It was March 2012. He had lost a leg three and a half years before and had endured hardships, depression and a suicide attempt. He had struggled with his reality. But now, he was a diver—an elite diver. He and his friends had big plans.

Chapter 4

"I am very grateful to be alive and to share my experiences. Especially here in Latin America, disability is the same as being a second- or third-class citizen, and you have no chance. We had a lot of work to do. I had cancer, but I am better now. I lost twenty-five percent of my body, but I can still do things. People don't understand what they can do. I am trying to change perceptions. I am having fun and enjoying life.

"When I lost my leg and felt sad and depressed, I wanted to share my message to inspire others. Facebook was new and I decided to set up an account. I had 200 friends in a blink, but it was all messed-up people. They were sending me naked pictures and things. I started to delete my account, but then I uploaded pictures with my wife and living a normal life. And then it started to grow. I have 5,000 friends and almost 2,000 fans on the fan page."

While his primary focus, and the point of Leo's efforts,

is to inspire people who have disabilities, his infectious sense of purpose has the same effect on the normally-abled as well.

"I am working with people who aren't disabled, but they still don't know what they can accomplish."

When you talk to Leo, he is gracious and humble about what he has done. He is even more so about what he plans to do. But that doesn't stop him from working at it every day. A lot of people in the world see injustice or trouble but very few work so hard to fix it.

Dr. J. Dario Gomez C, the Medical Director of Costamed Hyperbaric Chambers, DAN Medical Liaison for Mexico, and a DAN referral physician, served as Leo's medical advisor for both of his world-record dives.

"I believe Leo's message goal goes beyond scuba diving. Meeting him and talking to him serves as inspiration to anyone. To the disabled community, getting close to the beautiful world of diving delivers a great stimulus to their senses. Seeing the wonders of the underwater world, being weightless, and having the water surround them could be life changing."

Creating that life-changing opportunity is what it is all about—what this all comes down to for Leo.

"I want to make a point: the ocean gave me my life back. I learned how to face my life doing my scuba training. Being under the water with zero gravity is super cool. "My goal is to open a diving facility in Mexico and get people free from their wheelchairs and be relieved from their chains. At no cost."

Obviously, scuba diving has played an extremely important role in Leo's life, and he wants to share that experience with others. But, in general, he is trying to encourage others to live their lives and be exceptional.

"That moves me to send a message to people with disabilities that you have amazing things to do. Disability can be very cruel if you don't know how to fight it. I am pretty sure I am not going to change the world, but I can get the message out."

As with any endeavor like this, there are always going to be naysayers and doubters. Leo doesn't let that stop him, even when they have the completely wrong idea.

Leo suggested, "What if we set a world record?"

The quest to set a world record wasn't a mission to achieve fame. Or fortune. Leo wanted to set world-record dives for a person with a disability because he wanted to inspire others.

Often, the biggest ideas begin with a simple spark. Leo and Geman brainstormed about what they would need and how to get it. Leo had a few dive buddies, and they were all in immediately, but he knew he was going to need more help. They needed support and a team. The following week, German met with people from the diving industry in the area.

"He took me to the meeting and introduced me. He told them about me and asked if they wanted to support me. They all said, 'Let's do it!' And that's how it began. Everyone was so excited.

"About a month later, we had a meeting in Playa del

Carmen with the diving community. We asked for safety divers and a team to set the world record. We had four or five more divers who volunteered to help. These were the early first days.

"In July, we began training. We decided to train every Tuesday in Cozumel. For the next three months, we practiced.

"When I first started working on the record dives, people said, 'Leo is able to do these things because he is very rich and he has this prosthesis that the normal people do not have.' That's why in my professional images and in diving, I never use my prosthesis. The prosthesis is not me. I want people to see that what I do comes from the inside. I travel around the world, I have a beautiful life, I have a beautiful wife, and I do what I do. This is me now. This is Leo. I am not ashamed to show myself. I want people to understand they can do it, too. I would like to do more, but sometimes in Latin America, it seems like nothing is happening."

Leo described the days leading up to his first world-record dive as a quest. Everyone was motivated and excited. They planned to make the dive in December. Everyone on the team was a qualified technical diver with experience using the equipment they would need, but no one knew how to organize a dive team with a singular goal. They needed to work out the logistics of when team members would enter the water.

"I started to train every Tuesday for the sixteen weeks leading up to the dive. In the beginning, we all got in the water at the same time. It was cool, but it was a mess. We made a lot of mistakes. Tuesdays, we got together for the deep dives. I was diving four times a week, one day diving shallow, practicing drills and protocols. Practicing, practicing, practicing. I would practice in the cenotes diving against the current, to work on stamina and breathing."

A Mexican cenote is a water-filled cave system through the limestone bedrock. Over millions of years, fresh water has eroded the limestone, carving out complex cave systems. When the top of the cave falls in and opens access to the labyrinth below, it becomes a swimming hole or a dive destination.

The plan for this world-record dive was simple. They were going to make a statement with a deep dive. The biggest challenge for the dive was the location. Everyone on the team lived in Cozumel or elsewhere in Quintana Roo, Mexico.

The area is a diving mecca, blessed with warm water and good visibility. For many, another feature of the local diving is the strong ocean currents that surround the area. Divers typically make "drift dives" where they enter the water at one location and then drift along with the current, barely expending any energy. The dive boat follows along and picks them up when they reach their exit point or run low on air. This works fine for recreational divers who want to drift along a coral reef and see the sights. It is a bigger problem when a group of divers wants to stay together in the water and in one place for safety and control. Getting to depth is only a small part of the dive. Returning to the surface would be a longer and more challenging proposition.

During training, Leo and his team made it to 100 meters (330 feet) of seawater.

"That is a respectable number, but I wanted to do something more spectacular. I wanted to hit 150 meters (500 feet). I wanted to send a message. German said I could do it, but there was no other record for a diver with a disability, so, he said there was no reason to go 150 meters."

They agreed to aim for 122 meters (400 feet) of seawater for the world-record dive.

But making a dive to those depths takes planning and coordination. It also takes equipment. For one thing, air itself becomes toxic at those depths. Divers have to breathe trimix for their own safety. In the case of trimix for deep dives, helium is used to reduce the concentration of nitrogen and oxygen. A buildup of the nitrogen leads to decompression sickness and oxygen at-depth can cause seizures, an event potentially fatal underwater. The conflict, though, is that divers can't breathe the gas with the reduced oxygen content on the surface, either, because they would lose consciousness. This means they have to carry air, oxygen, and trimix with them on the dive and switch from one to the other at the appropriate time.

Decompression sickness happens when nitrogen bubbles form in the body following a dive. These bubbles expand in the bloodstream and in the body tissues, as the diver ascends, cutting off blood flow and causing pain. In serious cases, the bubbles form on the spinal cord, causing neurological problems including paralysis and death. Decompression sickness can happen to recreational divers on relatively shallow dives, swimming along a reef. Even divers who follow all of the rules of diving run a slight risk of decompression sickness on every dive.

The risk is higher for technical divers making dives like the one Leo planned. They would have to use trimix for the dive, switching from normal air at the surface to the trimix once they reached a prescribed depth, and then eventually switching to pure oxygen once they neared the surface following the dive. The ascent itself would take hours as the divers would have to ascend to predetermined depths and pause for a minute or two, allowing the accumulated nitrogen to be released from the body, before ascending to the next depth and repeating the process all over again. These dives took time and money.

"We dived four dives a month to those depths. It was a lot of money for the helium and the ferries. We used our own money. We didn't know anything about fundraising or preparing for a world record. There were eleven people on the team. We trained for six months."

Leo quickly discovered very few disabled divers did technical dives like he proposed and even less was written about it. They had to learn as they went. Some of the immediate concerns were that Leo's surgery and radiation therapy might have compromised his circulatory system, making it harder for his body to remove the nitrogen buildup in his system. The concerns were all theoretical because there was no research on the subject and little practical experience.

"I don't think Leo was at any higher risk. He wasn't in treatment at the time. As a diver, he surpassed any challenge and that's why he holds the level of certifications he has. His skills as a diver are better than the general diving population," Dr. J. Dario Gomez C said. "I was invited by Leo to be his medical advisor on the two records on Cozumel. I shared with him and the rest of the team my views on dive safety. We took the necessary measures and planning to minimize risks."

For a dive like this, you would normally lower a line with safety tanks. This gives you a point of reference underwater. Because of the current in Cozumel, that was impossible. Below 300 feet, the current gets especially strong. During their workup dives, they had to develop a system with a shallow support team and deep divers who stayed with Leo to keep him safe. Leo felt the entire dive was an exploration of his capabilities, the exact point he was trying to make.

According to Dr. Gomez, "Deep diving demands vast amounts of knowledge, experience, and discipline as well as appropriate preparation and equipment, since it is fraught with potential hazards. Deep diving poses problems that can be deadly at 120 meters (400 feet), such as hypercapnia, oxygen toxicity, nitrogen narcosis, and decompression illness. On top of that, some of the psychological and physiological effects vary from person to person and even from day-to-day. Variables can be very difficult to measure."

The project took on a life of its own when Leo's friend, Cesar Zepeda, met with a reporter. Needing something to write about, she asked Cesar to tell her a story. Cesar told her about the world-record dive project but then forgot to tell Leo about the conversation.

"The following day, I was training in the gym, and I started getting text messages that said things like 'Hey, you're famous.' But I didn't know about it. They gave me a half page in the Quintana Roo newspaper."

The first article in the state newspaper got things rolling.

"Everyone started calling me. In one blink, all the local media called me. Then, the director of tourism for Cozumel called and said they wanted to help by promoting diving on the island during the diving festival in December. They wanted to collaborate."

The story took off. The national media picked it up and then the Reuters news agency contacted him. The owners of the ferry company serving Cozumel and the mainland contacted him. They were finally getting some support for the project. Inevitably, not everyone was excited about the idea.

"When the diving community found out what we were doing, the old divers said, 'You are not able to do it. You are going to kill yourself, and you are going to embarrass the diving community. We will suffer the consequences. It is going to be a disaster.' I was very determined to make this dive happen. I knew I could do it."

German Yañez agreed they would move forward, but he cautioned they needed to be professional about everything they did.

"We had to design logistics to handle every possible situation and make sure we had plans for everything. As things got closer and more organized, it also got more exciting. It was super cool and super fun," recalls Leo.

Leo knew he needed a dive-industry sponsor. During training and practice dives, the dive team used borrowed and personal gear, which wasn't always up to the challenge.

"We were worried it was all old and used."

Leo knew he needed more help but wasn't sure where to get it.

"I went to the DEMA (Diving Equipment & Marketing Associates) show in November in Las Vegas. I wanted to know if there was anyone doing what I was doing. I had no money and didn't know anyone there. The day before the show, I sat in my house and said, 'If I want to win, I have to risk.' That morning, I bought my plane ticket to DEMA with the last of my money. I had no money for a hotel. I called my wife and said, 'I am leaving.' She asked, 'You're leaving where?' I told her what I was planning and the decision I had made. I told her, 'It is a leap of faith. Something is telling me to go.'"

There are times having the faith to get started is all it takes.

"I got on the plane and saw friends. They told me to go with them and told me where they got a room for $25 a night."

Leo followed his friends to their hotel. When he explained to the woman behind the counter his situation, she told him she couldn't book the cheap room he asked about directly. And then she did something extraordinary.

"She took out her own phone and set up the reservation for me."

She got him a room for $19 a night. But then she said she didn't have the cheap room and gave him a suite instead. Leo slept well and then got up early the next morning to attend the show.

DEMA is an annual trade show for the scuba diving industry. Equipment manufacturers, training agencies, and diving destinations set up to show off their latest products. Only dive professionals or other representatives from the dive industry are able to attend. The show is not open to the public.

"I walked to the convention center from my hotel. It was about two miles. At the show, I didn't have a badge to enter the show. It was expensive and I couldn't afford it."

Serendipity would again come into play. In the lobby of the show, Leo ran into his contact from the Cozumel Tourism Board. He explained his problem and what he was trying to do. The man immediately arranged for Leo to get a badge and attend the show.

"It was my first time at the show and I was excited. I was like a kid in a candy store," he said. "And then I got scared. I thought, 'I am nobody. Why would any of these important people care what I am trying to do?' I went to a coffee shop and called my wife. I told her I was coming home. She told me to relax and to not give up. She told me to give myself a chance."

Leo pulled himself together and returned to the show floor. As he walked around, he ran into some of his diving friends.

"I saw Alessandra Figari, and she walked with me to find sponsors and disabled diving organizations. She took me to the Poseidon Booth and introduced me to the CEO at the booth. His name was James Robertson."

Robertson was heading to a meeting but set up a meeting with Leo at 8:00 a.m. the next morning in the coffee shop at the Venetian Hotel. Leo and Alessandra tried to find the location the next day but never could. They missed the meeting.

"I said, 'Well that's it. We lost it.'"

He wasn't quite ready to give up, though, and went straight to the show floor. Leo found James Robertson as he finished another meeting. Leo apologized for missing him, and James told him he had ten minutes before his next appointment.

"He asked what I needed and I told him the gear I needed for the dive. He agreed to help me."

From there, Leo walked the show floor and confirmed what he had already suspected.

"I met with the disabled training people and found no one was doing what I was doing. No one was doing technical diving for people with disabilities."

DEMA was confirmation for Leo that he was headed in the right direction. He made new friends across the industry. He also learned an important lesson for this project and the ones that came after.

"A lot of people took care of me. They took me to lunch and dinner. I just had to have a little faith. If you have faith and the will to do something, the rest is excuses. I did it with a good intention and a good smile. If you jump in the current, the water will do half the work to move you along," he said. "Go and do the task."

Faith is an interesting subject when it comes to Leo.

"After the university, I wasn't a faithful man. But after the cancer, I started to think there had to be something else.

"Too many good things have happened to me. I am now a man of faith. I'm not religious, but I do believe in God, and things are happening, doors are opening, and it is too much to be a coincidence. After the surgery, I had to realize my potential. I am a better person than I used to be. I know myself and I know how capable I am. I understand about love and purity. I am more aware of love and all the good things in my life. If I had the chance to not lose my leg now, I would say no. While I didn't choose to lose my leg, it has motivated me to be the best person I can be. Everyone should be the best version of themselves."

Chapter 5

December 5, 2012, dawned clear and bright. The air was warm and humid with a slight breeze, like most days in Cozumel. But those perfect conditions couldn't distract Leo from what was going on. The last forty-eight hours leading up to the dive were stressful. He realized all the eyes of the world were looking at him.

"It was a lot of responsibility. I couldn't sleep that night."

Before the dive, the team had gotten together to review last-minute details and plans. Leo's mind focused on the seriousness of what they were doing, and he realized the magnitude of the event. The last thing he wanted to do was to let anyone down or set his cause back. Should he be injured or unable to complete the dive, it would leave the door open for people to question whether divers with disabilities could do what he was attempting. And, if they couldn't, he felt his failure could hurt all people with disabilities. He had set out to prove a person with a disability should have the same opportunities as anyone else. His success would help send that message. His failure would send the exact opposite message.

"The last month before the dive was stressful. People asked me if I was scared. Definitely, I was scared. People told me not to do it because I would kill myself. During the training, I hit 122 meters (400 feet) twice. The first time I was scared because I didn't know what to expect. I realized I was alone and how tiny I was. There are so many things that could go wrong, but the message and the reason you are doing it is powerful. That's what made me keep going. We didn't tell anyone we made it because we were waiting for the record."

Aside from the stress of the dive itself, the small size of the team putting this dive together put additional pressure on Leo. The last two weeks before the dive, Leo dealt with the media and logistics. Everyone wanted to talk to him and get the story. Leo knew the necessity of the interviews and the time spent talking to people, but it took him away from his preparation for the dive itself.

Leo was ready to get in the water and do what he had been preparing for the last six months. It was time to make the dive.

"I showed up early to get ready. Larena was with me all the time."

Leo's parents were there, too. It struck him how important his parents were to him and how much he relied on them.

"They were divorced, but on the day of the first record dive, they were both there on the boat. I didn't know if I would survive much longer. They forgot their differences and were there to support me."

Looking around at the crowd on the water was disconcerting. The dive team had invited many local divers to witness the dive. Others showed up on their own.

"I started to get scared because of all the divers who were invited to watch us. I was worried about my team exceeding their capabilities and getting hurt. It was like a kindergarten with divers everywhere.

"Five minutes before the dive, on the boat, we did a last briefing. This was the time to cancel any dive for any reason if there was a problem. No one spoke up. German prayed for the team. I said a prayer myself for the lives of the team members. There would be no point in doing this if anyone got hurt on the dive. From there, I can't remember anything but the dive. I was so focused. The next thing I knew, I was jumping in the water.

"I realized I had a lot of reasons to come back. My parents and wife gave me more reasons to be careful and safe. I wanted to send a powerful message and tell the disabled to reach for it and that they can do anything, but watching both of my parents in the same place was like, 'Wow! This is serious. I need to be very careful about this thing.'"

The primary deep dive team consisted of Leo, German Yañez, and Oliver Prats. The team worked perfectly. The three men made it to 122 meters (400 feet) of seawater. Then German and Oliver leveled off and allowed Leo to descend another four meters (12 feet) to set a clear record and be the deepest diver on the dive. Using full face masks and underwater communications, the divers spoke to each other and to their support divers who remained shallower.

"When I crossed the 125-meter (400-foot) depth, everyone signaled all was good. A friend at 90 meters (300 feet) started singing 'La Cucaracha.' I thought I was going crazy or poisoned by the breathing gas. And then I heard cheering and realized they were happy and it was all okay."

Still underwater, they shook hands and hugged.

With the depth record set, the dive wasn't over yet. Now came the more difficult part of returning to the surface slowly to avoid decompression sickness. The ascent required 25 decompression stops. Their first stop was at 76 meters (250 feet) and then they stopped every 3 meters (10 feet) above that for at least 1 minute. They made the dive to 125 meters (412 feet) in 12 minutes, but it took almost 3 hours to get to the surface. Support divers waited at 76 meters (250 feet) for the first stop and then a second team was there to meet them at 27 meters (90 feet). They rejoined the support teams: Leo, German, and Oliver always had a support diver with them in case a problem arose. Those divers brought additional breathing gas cylinders with them for the longest stops in the water. (See Appendix A: Dive Team for December 5, 2012 World-Record Dive for a complete list of divers on the dive team.)

"We all got together at twenty or thirty feet. It was one of the finest experiences of my life. The first person I looked for was my wife. She swam over and said, 'We did it!' and I said, 'Thanks to God!' Everyone was crying in the water."

Larena said, "The day Leo completed the world-record depth dive was a wonderful day. The sun shone on the island of Cozumel; the sea was totally calm. It was as if God made everything perfect for him to perform this feat. The atmosphere was full of optimism and friends. Many people accompanied us. When the dive began, I was very excited, a little nervous but very confident. He had trained for several months, and I knew he had reached his goal on more than one occasion. The wait was long, especially when you are waiting to see a loved one again. When the buoys began to emerge, everyone was excited and they announced Leo was about to leave the water. I jumped into the sea without thinking and swam to where he was. I hugged him, crying with happiness because he had fulfilled a big dream for him and for many people. We had a very special kiss, between happiness and gratitude, that everything had gone well, thanks to God."

A success, Leo received tremendous media attention for the dive, touching more than 200 million people worldwide. The publicity and support he received through his social networks told him he was on the right track. It motivated him to keep going. He immediately began planning his next challenge.

Chapter 6

The reaction to the first dive was swift and unanimous. Leo received notes of congratulations from around the world. But time was running out. Leo wanted to keep moving and working so he could serve his purpose before the cancer took him.

"My first motivation was the possibility that I would die very soon. They only gave me five years. My cancer didn't react well to radiation or chemo.

"When we did the first world record, my clock was ticking. I was thinking I would die before 2013. I had a strong desire to leave a legacy. I wanted to say to everyone to never surrender until the last breath. I was doing body scans every six months. My mind was playing tricks. My deadline was the five-year anniversary of the surgery. I wasn't making long-term plans. I was doing my best to be with my family and friends. I wasn't expecting to live that long. It was all mental.

"When we made the first world record, I thought, 'We sent a message. Disabled people can do amazing things.' Social media was an avalanche. I was befriended by people who were disabled and struggling with cancer. They said, 'What you did was so inspiring. Now I know I don't have to give up.' It was shocking to me to see the number of people whose lives were influenced by that dive."

Leo quickly discovered it wasn't just people with disabilities who were impressed with his world-record dive. He heard from family members of the disabled as well.

"All of them were saying, 'Do something again. We want to hear more about you.'"

As a result, Leo was the focus of a documentary based on that first dive—*Leo Morales: A Warrior's Story.*

In January, February, and March, Leo did a lot of media interviews. He was asked to be part of another documentary, *The Current* with Jean-Michel Cousteau. In March 2013, a video crew came to Cozumel to interview him.

"I was really enjoying the event because I met a veteran from Iraq and Afghanistan and some other disabled athletes. It was all about how the ocean healed our wounds and gave us back our lives. It was great to work with Cousteau."

Leo planned his next feat. There was no point in going deep again. With his team, Leo decided to make a long-distance dive—to dive the entire Cozumel marine park. The marine park is twenty kilometers wide with twenty-three diveable reefs. To his knowledge, no one had ever dived all twenty-three reefs in one dive, disabled or otherwise.

The first idea was to make the dive using open-circuit scuba, like he had used on the first dive, but they quickly determined that wouldn't be practical. They estimated it would take eighty scuba cylinders for Leo and his support team. He would personally have to use at least a dozen. The other option was to make the dive using dive technology Leo had never used before: rebreathers. It would take a lot of training just to get started preparing for this dive.

In some ways, scuba diving rebreather systems are old technology come full circle. Some of the earliest self-contained underwater breathing devices, prior to the advent of Jacques Cousteau and Emile Gagnan's Aqualung, were rebreathers.

Open-circuit scuba means the diver's exhaled breath is vented to the ocean. Each inhalation comes directly from the scuba cylinder through a regulator that delivers the breathing gas at a pressure slightly above ambient. The air is fresh and clean, and the diver is able to breathe easily, regardless of the depth.

Rebreathers are closed-circuit devices. The diver's exhaled breath is kept in a continuous loop. The rebreather unit scrubs out the exhaled carbon dioxide and adds in small amounts of oxygen back into the circuit. This system is more efficient and can last significantly longer on a single dive, typically up to four to five hours. The other advantage of a rebreather system is modern electronic controls can make sure the diver is breathing the appropriate gas mix, regardless of the depth. On Leo's first dive, he had to switch breathing gasses from air when he began his descent to "bottom gas" when he reached a certain depth and then switch again when he was doing his staged decompression afterward.

As with anything, there are trade-offs. Rebreather systems are significantly more expensive than open-circuit units. The user also must have hours of specialized training in the specific rebreather he or she plans to use. Most importantly, they require strict attention to how they are set up. If the scrubber unit is not configured properly, the carbon dioxide in the diver's exhale will begin to build up in the circuit, causing him or her to lose consciousness.

Through his contacts, Leo reached out to Nautilus Rebreathers. Casey Omholt agreed to help him on this dive and supplied Leo with five units for the team's use. Leo was back in training with a new goal.

"We got in touch with the marine park administration and began researching depths and currents to plot out the course for the dive. I started to train in July 2013 when we got the units. I never used a rebreather before this. Even shallow, it demanded a lot of training. We had to find a way to eat and drink water while underwater. We had to develop the logistics of this complex dive."

Complex was right. By its very nature, this dive was going to be dramatically different than the first one. Instead of staying in one spot, the boats were going to cruise through the marine park slowly. They planned the entire dive at only 12 meters (40 feet) of seawater, so decompression issues were not big, even though they planned to spend hours underwater. But they were going to have to find a way to stay at the same depth throughout the dive: not an easy task. The terrain below Leo would change significantly and the exceptional visibility around Cozumel would make it hard to judge depth by looking around you. At first, they thought Leo was going to have to pay close attention to his depth gauge throughout the dive. He had to be very precise about his depth because variations would change the amount of time he could spend underwater. The pressure differential of just a meter (a few feet) might not make a big difference in the short term, but over eight or more hours they anticipated the dive would take, it could change the effectiveness of the scrubber unit. Each unit would give him four to five hours underwater, so he was going to have to switch from one unit to a second complete rebreather unit while submerged. They planned to swim a replacement rebreather down to Leo and have divers help him switch the units out underwater.

"It is easy to get confused about depth. I dived a little overweighted and then attached a line to a big buoy on the surface to a D ring on my rebreather unit. I was actually hanging from the buoy. That was how I stayed at 12 meters (40 feet)."

Having Leo hang from the surface buoy underwater also served as a safety device.

When you are diving a rebreather, especially for a long period, there is always a chance of a buildup of CO_2.

None of them have active CO_2 sensors. That is always a risk. If, at any time, he lost consciousness, the buoy would keep him from sinking to the bottom. It would also make it easier for the rescue team to bring him to the surface. The weight of the rebreather unit itself is comparable to wearing open-circuit double tanks, that is 40 kilos (80 to 100 pounds) of equipment.

The current in Cozumel can be tricky. Sometimes, it helps you and sometimes it pushes against you. He had to be very careful since he would be free swimming using the current.

Dr. Gomez was again asked to serve as the medical advisor for this dive.

"Distance diving in this case was at a safe depth for DCS. But it brought many other challenges. The one we could control easily was O_2 toxicity, as the rebreather mix was calculated in a very safe way. The power autonomy of the rebreather, water temperature, daylight and physical exertion were also taken in account. Psychologically for Leo, it was a very special day as it marked the five-year anniversary of his life expectancy. So this could have played a great role in the effort he made that day."

Another issue they faced was how to move through the water. Considering the distance, Leo and his team considered using underwater diver propulsion vehicles, called scooters, to be able to complete the entire dive in four or five hours. They contacted a number of scooter manufacturers, but no one was interested in supporting the dive.

"We didn't want to keep them. They didn't want to be liable or have the bad publicity. That's how life is. I was getting discouraged, and I explained the situation to Alessandra. She told me not to use a scooter since I was a disabled person sending a message. People would say the scooter did the work, not me.

Alessandra was right. The goal of the dive wasn't for Leo to take a ride and travel a distance using technology and equipment. It was about him making the dive using his own body power. They decided to continue the project without a scooter.

"We wanted to prove the human body had no limits. We decided that would be a more powerful message."

Another logistical question came from finding a way to drink water underwater. They tried a number of options but settled on an easy solution.

"We filled a plastic bag with water and squeezed it. The simplest thing in the world is always best."

After they learned how to use the Nautilus Rebreather units, they practiced and spent time in the water to get used to diving for hours at a time.

"We trained a lot for four months, moving from one hour to five hours at time. I was practicing diving with a marker buoy on the surface and a boat following me.

"As I was getting more training and learning more about diving, Robert Stevens, the PADI Regional Manager for Mexico, invited me to become a PADI Open Water Scuba Instructor. He did eventually become a PADI scuba instructor, meeting the full criteria just the same as a diver who had all four limbs. He was now fully certified to train anyone to dive, disabled or not.

———————

Cesar Zepeda supported Leo and planned to dive with Leo the whole time. The day before the dive, they realized they had a problem. Nautilus provided them with five dive units. But when they checked them out a final time before the dive, two of them weren't working correctly. And replacement parts were too far away to get there the next morning in time for the planned world-record dive attempt. They were going to have to change their plans.

Three rebreather units were the minimum they needed for Leo to make the dive. They had to keep one unit in reserve for emergencies. Unfortunately, that meant Cesar was not able to make the dive with Leo as they had planned. An even bigger concern was they didn't have a plan in place for support divers and there was no way Leo was going to be able to make the dive alone. It would not be safe.

"A friend who is a commercial diver, in Los Cabos, Mexico, Roberto Perez, came for the dive. He said we couldn't do this since there wasn't a support diver."

The commercial diver set up a system of six dive teams so there would be two divers in the water at all times. Each team would dive with Leo for forty-fifty minutes and then be relieved by the next team. He made it all work perfectly.

Runners training for marathons do not typically run 26.2 miles when they train. In the same way, Leo had never dived for 8 or 10 hours on a dive. He had practiced the equipment switches underwater and knew those drills backward and forward, but he had never made a dive longer than 5.5 hours. His team had agreed there was no reason to dive longer. The equipment change was unique, as well. Rebreather divers practice bailout drills underwater so they know what to do in case there is an equipment failure while underwater, but as far as they knew, no one was changing out rebreather units underwater.

"I was nervous that day because I didn't know what to expect. I knew it would be hard, but the second half of the dive was going to be something new for me."

Leo knew his parents did not understand the greater risks involved in this technical dive. His mom was naïve about it all and his father would say, "Be safe; don't do stupid things."

Leo was nervous, but he was having fun when he finally jumped in the water on December 13, 2013. There were a lot of expectations and pressure on him, in the media and social media. The slogan for the dive was "20,000 Meters Under the Sea," giving a nod to Jules Verne's *20,000 Leagues Under the Sea*.

Just like running a marathon, this dive was about endurance, both physical and mental. Leo had to keep swimming and keep focused, long after he got tired.

"After hour six, I started to hallucinate. I imagined I was alone. I had support divers around me, but I thought

I was alone. I thought everyone left me," Leo said. "I had talked to friends who ran marathons, and they said it was perfectly normal. I looked up and couldn't see the boats. We had eight to ten boats following me. We had support boats from the marine park, from the navy for evacuations and two or three more, but I couldn't see them. The mind can be really tricky."

After he got past the hallucinations, he came back to reality and saw people around him. He wasn't alone. Although Jean-Michel Cousteau had come to Mexico for Leo's second dive to show *The Current* at the Cozumel dive festival, ScubaFest, he had also planned to visit Leo underwater. Ear problems prevented him from diving. However, Edwin Corona replaced Cousteau. Corona is one of the oldest divers in Mexico, a legend in the diving world, who doesn't dive regularly anymore due to his health. He was 73 at the time of the dive. Seeing a legend swimming down to support him gave Leo the boost he needed.

"Corona jumped into the water with me even though he doesn't dive anymore. That woke me up. He was there with a team. He motivated me to keep going. That encouraged me to keep going."

The boost lasted a while, but by hour seven, Leo was beginning to wear out.

"I said, 'I quit, I'm done. I just want to go up.'"

Leo's friend and technical diving instructor German Yañez was the support diver at this time.

"German looked me in the eyes and wrote a message on a slate, stating there were a lot of people waiting for me. If I wanted to quit, I could because I had already set a record. He reminded me not to think about all the people waiting. I had already stopped kicking and given up. But then I thought of all the people. He wrote that moments like these were where legends were made."

Leo agreed to keep going, but he was exhausted and had nothing left in reserve. He wrote to German he needed something to give him energy. When they passed the message back to the surface, Leo's wife, Larena, remembered she was carrying a tiny bottle of honey in her purse.

"They sent it down to me in a plastic bag. I squeezed it into my mouth, and it was like an injection of pure adrenaline. I was able to keep swimming another hour and fifteen minutes."

Finally, the current turned against him, and he barely moved through the water. He was breathing hard from the exertion and the exhaustion. He could tell the carbon dioxide levels in his breathing circuit were getting high. After a disabled friend with polio from Spain, Jose Gomez, and his support diver, Vicente Fito, jumped into the water to dive with him along with champion Mexican freediver, Alejandro Lemus Nava, they decided to finish the dive together.

When they were done, they stopped short of the goal of 20 kilometers, swimming15.6 kilometers. While he didn't swim the entire marine park, the dive covered almost 10 miles and lasted 8 hours and 16 minutes.

"I dedicated this dive to two special divers. Sergio Cavalero, who was struggling with pancreatic cancer, and Jose Gomez. They had waited for me for more than eight hours. German Yanez, the surface coordinator, told everyone to get in the water. We had a big party." (See Appendix B: Dive Crew for 2013 World-Record Dive.)

Chapter 7

Twice Leo Morales had pushed his body to the very limits of human endurance. He had dived deeper and longer than anyone with a disability and deeper and longer than all but a handful of divers in general.

The question is why? Why push himself? Why risk death or further injury? Why put in the long hours training and practicing? Why take the risks and put in the personal investment?

The answer for Leo was that he knew life would have killed him faster. It is likely he would already be dead. Even in the midst of his training and goals and public appearances, he struggled with depression and bouts where he felt like he was less of a man. He wasn't immune to those feelings.

He fights them every day. Most days he is successful, but it is still a fight. Leo knows two things. First, he is lucky to be able to do what he does and second, he has an obligation to keep pushing, to keep inspiring and to keep sending a message. In the same way, his message is twofold. First, he wants to tell other people with disabilities, whether they have lost a limb or have a medical condition that makes them "different" that they can do whatever they want to do. His constant refrain is, "Nothing is impossible!" In spite of his own struggles, physical and mental, he has continued to work to make sure everyone in the world knows physical limitations don't have to be limitations at all. And that speaks to the second part of his message. He wants to tell people who don't have disabilities that they don't have the right to look down on someone who is different than they are.

Not every country has laws and protections to fight against discrimination. And even the places that do have them don't always enforce them. More often, people or companies willing to discriminate against those with disabilities are subtler. They don't come right out and say what they are thinking, they hide behind excuses. Ultimately, it serves the same purpose and achieves the same result.

"I'm not doing this for me, I'm doing it to change the world. We never said it would be easy or with no risk, but it is coming from the bottom of our hearts."

At the press conference following the second world-record dive, he said, "In order to make it special, we had to make it powerful. I want to change the perception of disability."

Knowing he was pushing the boundaries of human endurance didn't stop Leo from his quest, either. "I had no diving insurance and no health insurance would cover me during the dives. If I had gotten hurt, the expense for the medical care would have fallen entirely on my shoulders. None of the insurance companies was willing to accept the risk. I knew what I was doing, but the message was more important to me. We succeeded in sending a message. It was crazy, it was risky, but it was a blank page of what disabled divers and cancer survivors can do."

Leo even surrounds himself with others who are facing challenges. One of his safety divers has diabetes. His doctor told him that he couldn't dive because of his risk for losing consciousness. Leo said the man is one of his best shallow support divers. (If a person with diabetes were to have a blood sugar crash in the water, he could lose consciousness underwater. The risk of drowning is greatly increased at that point, and it also raises the risk of the diver's buddy getting injured while trying to perform an in-water rescue and bring the unconscious diver to the surface. Note: In 2005, the diving medical community came together and worked out a set of guidelines that would allow divers with diabetes to safely dive.)

And while no one takes anything away from him that he didn't make the full 20 kilometers of the dive, and he concedes it was still a powerful statement, he would like to try it again. Leo doesn't like to leave anything unfinished.

Leo's dream has been to create a place where others can come and experience the ocean in the same way he has.

"The ocean gave me my life back and I want to bring more people to the ocean."

Since he completed the second world-record dive, Leo has been working to establish a foundation and create a program to bring disabled divers to the water.

"I want to make Playa del Carmen or Cozumel, Mexico, a destination for disabled divers from around the world. We will have the facilities they need to experience the underwater world and the freedom it gives them."

While the physical aspects of moving and staying active are important to people with disabilities, Leo also realizes firsthand that the mental aspects are just as important. When you consider someone who is as upbeat and motivated as Leo is and how easy it is for him to get frustrated or depressed at the things he has had to endure, it is obvious that this project isn't a simple, one-step process.

"We need to help them rehabilitate their minds."

With the money his planned facility generates as a dive destination for disabled divers, he plans to bring people with disabilities from the local community to learn to dive for free. He wants them to experience what he has experienced, especially considering the discrimination he knows is present in Mexico.

The road to providing diving opportunities has been frustrating, though. In spite of his worldwide notoriety and the attention his feats have brought to disabled diving and diving in Mexico, he has struggled to get the people who can help him to follow through on their offers of help.

"I've gotten a lot of empty promises from politicians and businessmen in the local community."

Even after his successes, Leo got depressed again in 2014 after fighting with people to help him help out the community.

"I've been trying to put together these empty promises. The people who can make this happen aren't doing anything. I was saying nothing is going on in Mexico. I decided not to wait. I started organizing events to keep it moving. I decided to move forward in the United States first."

Leo is obviously a person and a diver. But he also knows he is a public figure and an inspiration. He thinks of himself, in a professional sense, in three ways:

1. The athlete and the sports figure

2. The foundation, helping people and doing social work

3. Source of income to support his family

Those three parts make up a three-legged stool. They support each other and make up the whole. For example, to further his goals to help others and to earn an income, Leo has branched out, giving presentations about his experiences and the two world-record dives.

"I am in the process of learning how to combine those three aspects of my career. I really need an agent to help get financial support and sponsors. I know it is difficult because we've been through this twice."

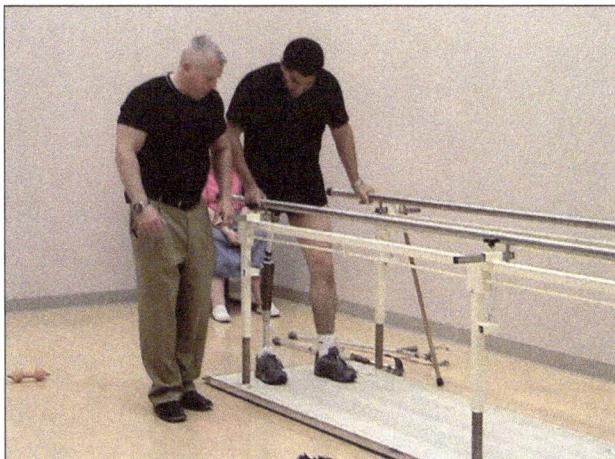

First steps: Leo takes his first steps in his new prosthesis with Stan Patterson. *Photo courtesy of Stan Patterson.*

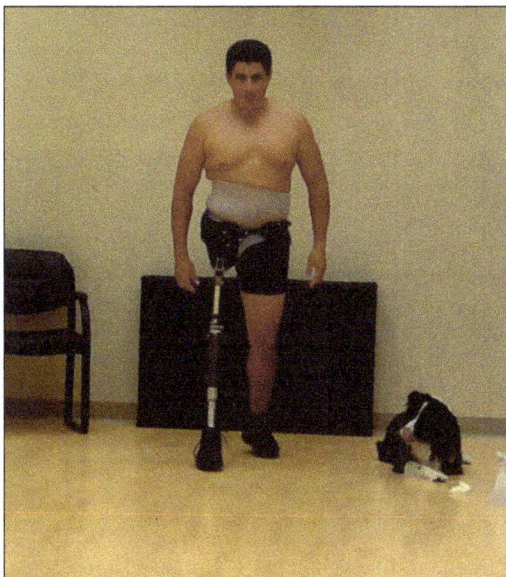

Standing on his own: Leo learns to stand and walk unaided with his prosthesis at POA.
Photo courtesy of Stan Patterson.

After the dive: Leo is all smiles after a dive in a Mexican cenote near his home in Playa del Carmen.

Finding freedom: The weight of the world has been removed when Leo is diving. *Photo courtesy of Marcel Gubern.*

First kiss: Larena Morales gives Leo a kiss when he reaches the surface following his first world-record dive.
Reprinted with permission from Norberto O. Bermúdez.

Silent world: Leo enjoys the peace and beauty of a coral reef near his home. Diving opened the world to Leo.

Job done: Leo decompresses from the dive on his way to the surface following his world-record dive to 125 meters (412 feet).

Final stop: Leo and his support dive team make a final stop before completing the world-record deep dive for a person with a disability. The dive required different breathing gases for every stage.

Final preparations: Leo takes a moment to check his dive computers before starting his swim across the Cozumel Marine Park.

Making the swim: Leo and a support diver swim across the Cozumel Marine Park. Leo is diving with a Prism rebreather.

In training: Leo had never dived a rebreather before deciding to use one in his second world-record dive. It required training and hours of practice to get ready for the dive.

Chapter 8

Scuba diving is an unforgiving and unnatural sport. The very act of breathing underwater usually takes a few minutes for most beginning divers to get used to. Using the proper equipment and training, divers can explore the ocean and feel microgravity, the closest to weightlessness you can get without joining the space program, all while seeing flora and fauna that look like something out of a science fiction movie. At the same time, mistakes can quickly get divers in trouble under-water. Finding yourself 12 or 15 meters (40 or 50 feet) underwater (or deeper) without an air supply or a mask to see through is terrifying. Even the most experienced divers can sometimes grow complacent, taking liberties with their preparation or the safety rules and then get themselves in trouble.

It takes a lot of self-confidence to face the challenges Leo has faced over the last few years. He has faced cancer, radiation therapy, depression, and a suicide attempt. He has handled the pressure of extreme depths and the greater pressure of thousands of pairs of eyes watching his every move. Some of those watchers expected him to fail. Others prayed he wouldn't. That pressure molds a man. Living through it and handling it successfully can give an extra boost of confidence.

In the summer of 2015, Leo was asked to participate in a photo shoot for Cressi with the Mexican freediver, Alejandro Lemus Nava. Cressi is one of the oldest dive equipment companies in the world. It began in 1939, making freediving equipment in Italy before Jacques Cousteau's Aqualung.

"It was probably the worst diving experience in my life," he began.

Leo had contacted a friend to reserve a dive boat. The friend was supposed to set everything up and make sure they had everything in place. Leo was asked to serve as the "technical diver for the photo shoot." They wanted him in front of the camera to show the differences between freediving, recreational diving and technical diving.

"I ordered a set of doubles. We got to the boat, but the boat had only singles. I didn't bring my BCD for a single."

Leo had brought the gear and equipment he would need to dive as a technical diver with twin tanks. He didn't have the equipment he needed to make the dive with a single tank. The dive operation tried to find some. They waited two hours for the set of double tanks to arrive, but they never showed up. They had an appointment with the photographer for the shoot, so they couldn't reschedule.

"I told them to get me a BCD and a regulator and let's do it. It was better to have something rather than nothing."

The dive operation found Leo a BCD to use, but it was a medium. He wore an extra-large. However, he decided he could make it work.

Because they were running late and Leo felt like he was to blame for the delay, he rushed to get to the dive site and in the water.

"The divemaster was putting everything together for me. I didn't test it first. I jumped into the water and I was leaking from everywhere. I looked like an Alka-Seltzer™."

The low-pressure inflator to allow him to add air to the BCD from the tank wasn't working. He disconnected it. Under normal, recreational circumstances, a diver can manually inflate his BCD by taking his regulator out of his mouth and breathing air directly into a mouthpiece on the BCD. In this situation, though, Leo was diving with a full face mask like he used on his world-record dives. (A full face mask is a mask and regulator connected into one piece. There is an oral nasal pocket to breathe through your nose. This mask allows you to actually speak underwater.) Leo couldn't orally inflate the BCD without removing and flooding his entire mask. While it was possible to do all of that, it wouldn't be practical or efficient. This was especially important considering the delays they had already experienced.

"I told the divemaster about the leaks. He grabbed my gear and a couple of wrenches and tightened it up. He then jumped into the water with my gear to test it while

I was on my surface interval. The leaks had stopped. We finished our surface interval, but I didn't check the rest of my gear.

"We made the first dive in 12 to 15 meters (40 to 50 feet). For the second dive, we decided to go to the wreck. I hadn't been there in two years. The maximum depth was 24 meters (80 feet)."

Considering Leo's experience and training, dives between 12 and 24 meters (40 and 80 feet) were simple. In his mind, he could handle whatever happened, he just wanted to get through the photo shoot and help them get the photos they needed.

"This time I used a hood. My BCD wasn't working at all. Everyone was getting relaxed and I started to struggle. I realized something was wrong. I ascended to sixty feet. The air in the full face mask started to leak into my hood and water was in my mask. I pulled my full face mask off and switched to my backup regulator and tried to breathe, but there was nothing there. It wasn't working. I looked around and there was no one there. I was running out of air."

To give himself a little more time and a chance to get himself under control, Leo decided to orally inflate his BCD, since the full face mask was out of the way. But he didn't have the breath left in his lungs. He was in trouble. His body started to demand air and there was none to be had. He wasn't thinking clearly.

Panic is a process where your mind begins to spiral out of control, forgetting training and options until the only thing left to do is fight or flee. This is often called tunnel vision, as you can no longer see what is around you and your perceived options narrow down to one. For a diver, this is a problem. Making a panicked ascent from 18 meters (60 feet) underwater is an ideal way to lose consciousness and drown or possibly suffer a lung over-expansion injury.

"I started to inhale some water and I thought, 'This is the end.' I didn't even think to release my weight belt. I inhaled some water into my nose again. It was strange. I started to relax. My brain wasn't working properly."

As his thoughts raced, part of his training came back to Leo and he remembered to press the full face mask against his face and purge it. He hit the button to release air into the mask and was relieved when air started bubbling out. He swallowed some water, but he was able to breathe.

Since they were rushed, no diving safety officer had been assigned. No one had the job of watching the divers and making sure everyone was okay.

"No one realized I was in trouble. Another diver on the shoot, the girl with the GoPro, turned around and looked at me. She gave me an OK signal, asking if I was all right, and I signaled her, 'No.' She tried to give me an extra weight."

The diver thought Leo was having trouble staying underwater.

"I grabbed her backup regulator octopus and took a deep breath."

Leo finally resolved his problem and eventually made it back to the surface.

"I realize now how easy it is to get overconfident. I made a bunch of mistakes that day and I understand how easy it is for that to happen. I am very reflective now and try to go back to the basics."

While dive accidents are relatively rare events, there is very little margin for error. They often begin with a small problem that turns into panic that then turns into a disaster.

"It was scary. I really felt like I was drowning. You are never supposed to change the dive plan for any reason and I had made a lot of changes, from the dive plan to the gear I was using, without thinking through what that meant. You can get overconfident. I felt like I was invincible. I didn't take the problems seriously and check them out for myself. I just jumped into the water without checking out my gear myself."

After his diving "near miss," Leo has become more thoughtful about what he is doing and more reflective about his motivations. He fell into a trap that many highly trained divers and anyone who has achieved a great level of success at a technical endeavor can encounter.

"When you are learning about diving, you can begin to think you are capable of solving any problem. The lesson I learned was that you always have to remember that you are in an environment that can kill you in an instant. I think I was getting an ego and being overconfident. I was thinking, 'Nothing can happen to me. What could go wrong on a single tank dive?' I had the wrong attitude and I almost died. I didn't know I was getting to that point. I'm very grateful for the chance to look back at the real mission and my real purpose. It was a wake-up call.

"I was really scared. I thought I would die that day. But I am glad to have the chance to share my experience. This was a positive experience. I was getting overconfident and that is not good, especially below 300 feet. It taught me a great lesson. Not to be a maniac, but to double-check my gear and the procedure. I was getting lax."

This was the perfect reset as he prepared for the next step in his life: world-record dive #3.

Chapter 9

As Leo planned for his next world-record dive, he was asked to speak at the Cancun Rotary Club for the Young Rotarians on May 15, 2015. The following is an excerpt from his speech, which describes Leo's desire and efforts to use his own personal story to spread the word about disabilities and convey his beliefs that the only limits on what any of us can do are in the mind. There are events in life that appear to be devastating but, in reality, are the ones that generate great stories.

Dear Young Rotarians, Distinguished Family and Guests,

It is gratifying for me to have the opportunity to be heard and above all that I be allowed to tell you a story . . . my story.

You know the meaning of the phrase "having it all"? Of having everything we could ever want? Of the arrogance of pursuing things, material possessions, and status symbols?

Human beings naturally tend to pursue external happiness. We look for happiness in our work, financial stability, family, social status, home, cars and businesses. Everyone has their own definition of having it all. We form these ideas from our way of life, our upbringing, our needs, and our preferences. My definition of having it all and yours are likely very, very different.

But what happens when life itself has given you everything and suddenly decides that you must learn the greatest lesson by taking it "all" away and leaving you with nothing?

Suddenly, we are forced to think about the time, the effort, the hours of study, the lost sleep and lost money and the time that was dedicated to this pursuit and not to family. Is it okay to sink into an armchair and become depressed or try to find someone else to blame?

Let me tell you my life story. In 2008, my personal and professional life was in full ascent. I worked in the financial sector and at age twenty-eight became the youngest director of a bank in my region and won several awards for outstanding performance.

And then suddenly, on a day like any other day, my life turned 180 degrees without bothering to consult me. I began to feel discomfort in my lower back. At first, it was a small bother, but eventually it grew to become a constant pain. Finally, when the pain became intense and something I could no longer ignore, I saw a doctor. Of course, it was a bother for me to go see a doctor. When you have it all you never seem to have time to go to the doctor or take care of yourself.

I was shocked when the doctor told me I had a very advanced cancer. Imagine receiving this bit of news. It was devastating. The doctor told me the tumor weighed three kilos and covered the inside of my leg and right buttock. He also said there was a serious risk that it would spread to the rest of my body.

I thought nothing worse could happen. What could be worse than a three-kilo tumor in your body, right? Wrong. There were still more surprises left in store for me. After thoroughly analyzing my situation, the doctor told me my only option to continue living was to have my right leg amputated. Even worse, this was not the end of it. Even if I lived through the surgery, I could only expect to live for less than five years.

My family has always been supportive, and I was able to lean on them in this difficult time, but still it was not an easy situation. I was about to lose everything—a paradox in which I had to risk my life to save it. After much discussion with my family, I took a leap of faith, tossing my life into the unknown with very little chance of survival. The day of my surgery, I said goodbye to everyone and everything, knowing I would probably not wake up. I asked God for the opportunity to have one more day of life.

After eight hours of surgery, I woke up from the anesthesia. I took a deep breath. I was alive, but at the same time, I had a deep, unexplainable feeling that something wasn't right. Still half asleep, I could sense an empty space in the hospital bed where my right leg should have been. There was only a white sheet below me. I had lived through the surgery, but now I was physically incomplete.

The changes I faced inside were just as significant as the changes on the outside. I was now disabled. The world remained the same but not even my friends and family managed to understand the depression drowning me and running through my veins.

I spent the next year trying to adapt to my new reality. I had an incomplete body. I had to decide to cling to life. I had to accept my new fragility and continue moving forward. I had to relearn everything from walking to toileting. I had to sit and learn all the basic tasks we learn when we are young children. This was the most complete physical and mental challenge of my thirty-six years. I had to get around in a wheelchair or use crutches. I had to go to painful therapies and appointments with psychologists and psychiatrists to overcome my loss, knowing that all the work would not return my leg to me.

When I was ready to return to work, I suffered discrimination and was fired. I received settlement payments, but the frustration was indescribable. I devoted years to serve a company, guarding their own interests as if they were my own. And then, overnight, they didn't need me anymore. I give thanks that they did this, actually, because I could not work for a company that could not bear to have a man without a leg laboring for them. Obviously, they made this decision based on their public image. But losing my leg did not mean that I lost part of my brain and the intelligence that I used to give the company big profits.

Losing my job complicated everything even more. My beloved wife was dealing with a husband who focused on his own suffering. I was drowning in depression. She wanted to improve my condition, but I had to work on myself to get ahead. At the time, I was just alternating between denial and anger.

One day, a good friend invited me to go scuba diving as an alternative physical therapy to what I was doing. It took him a few hours to convince me, but I finally accepted his invitation. I had already been diving before, but as a kind of fun thing to do, never as a sport. Still, I already knew more or less what to expect.

Still, when I reached Puerto Aventuras, I was overcome with fear of the unknown. I felt a wild despair at being underwater and out of control. I hated my friend completely. I became depressed and cried inside my mask. I couldn't see anything through the tears. The other divers who accompanied me realized something was wrong and immediately took me to the surface. When I got out of the water, I was angry and frustrated. I didn't want to know anything about physical therapies. I didn't want to talk to anyone or leave my house.

My good friend William Lotz told me I needed to try it again. He kept insisting on it and after many weeks, I finally agreed to try diving again. The second time was much different. It took me a few minutes to get comfortable after I entered the water, but once I got my breathing under control and began to swim at a leisurely pace, I opened my eyes to a new world. This new world could be all mine. I was floating. I felt like an angel suspended in the sky. I felt alive! I was able to get around on my own. No wheelchair. No crutches. I didn't need the support of a friend. Again it was me who controlled my own movements. The sea with its colorful flora and infinite marine life received me with open arms. I felt alive!

Now take a minute . . . please . . . get up from your seat by yourself. Move. Walk one or two steps to stretch your legs. That's a feeling I'll never feel. I will never again be able to balance on two legs and feel the ground beneath my feet.

Life is full of special and valuable things. Too often we forget about those things and fail to enjoy them, to feel them, to appreciate them. Every day the sun rises is an opportunity to be better, to focus not on our weaknesses but on our strengths. It is a fact that I do not have and never will have my right leg, but I still have my other leg. I can still move around and find the best advantage of the day. And living every day makes it worth it. The choice is to see the glass half-full or half-empty.

Please take your seat and we'll continue with the story.

Hoping to continue diving and to repeat the experience of freedom I felt underwater, I started taking courses. Initially, these classes were a safety valve for me. I used them to prove to myself that I could do the same things as normal people. Gradually, I acquired certifications until almost without realizing it, I became a diving instructor. Let me tell you that there are very few disabled dive instructors. Later, I also became an instructor for people with disabilities. To challenge myself more, I became a technical diving instructor. This is the highest level of diving internationally. All this has allowed me to give lectures, set world records of diving for people with disabilities, receive prizes and participate in programs, both domestic and abroad. I don't just speak to audiences with disabilities but to people with full capabilities.

Over time, I realized that I may be physically challenged, but the real disability is in the mind!

Have you heard of the phoenix? It is part of the symbolism of alchemy, to represent rebirth through fire. This mythological bird, in the medieval legend of the phoenix, lives in Arabia but flies to Egypt to suffer its ritual death and regeneration. It is a purple or red bird that builds a pyre of wood and spices. The sun's rays light the fire and the bird fans the flame using its wings. It is consumed entirely by the fire. Then, a new phoenix rises from the ashes.

Humans can be reborn as many times as necessary. They can reinvent themselves!

Think about what happens in your life. The worst thing you can do is to actually stay in your comfort zone. You fall into a routine that is comfortable—or not always comfortable, but not so uncomfortable that you have to do anything about it. You get used to the stone in your shoe that hurts but does not kill you. You may have everything you think you need, or so you like to believe. If you do, you will never explore your true potential. That is the greatest risk. If you get stuck by your own choice, you never find out what you are capable of doing. Do not postpone your dreams because maybe when you decide to try something, it will be too late.

If something is not working in your life, delete it. Turn the page. It may make you uncomfortable to look at a blank canvas, but gradually you will start filling it in with what you want. Give it your personal touch. You will add colors and even textures. Break your barriers and reinvent yourself as many times as necessary.

I was forced to do this. I had to reinvent myself. I broke through the barriers, and I recognized diving could inspire me to live fully again. At the same time, I realized diving could inspire others. I realized my abilities, and I started visiting with people like me—people with disabilities. I discovered a passion that allowed me to move forward. I recognized life took something away from me but gave me something better.

Sometimes you have to lose everything to win it all.

Now, let me tell you a little about this sublime passion to bless my life—scuba diving. I can tell you diving is like the canvas where I can paint my feelings, the place where I can fly. I'm free. I have no ties and I can express myself completely. I can fully develop my abilities, and I'm not afraid to be myself. Scuba diving gives me complete freedom of movement. I can move in three dimensions and have contact with nature. It is also great exercise. Imagine how much the tanks and other equipment weigh. They are extremely heavy!

If you are interested in meditation, being underwater gives you the opportunity to be alone with your thoughts. It gives you time for introspection and reflection without distractions like the phone, tablet, TV or anything else.

In the last few years, I have dedicated myself to develop adapted scuba diving in Mexico through the foundation A Mar Abierto AC. My goal is to provide this feeling to those who need it. There are many arguments against this. It is difficult or dangerous. It is expensive to do something differently than we have always done it. These are all excuses that we use for not trying something new. As a side benefit, exposing more disabled and normally-abled people brings them to the natural wonders of our beautiful Mexico and the Caribbean Sea.

I would not have been able to do any of the things I have accomplished without an incredible team of divers. I have put my life in their hands and every decision we make involves the safety of the team. I have been the focus of these efforts, but I would not have been able to do any of these things without them. Working with them, I have set two world records for people with disabilities.

On December 8, 2012, I established the world record for deep diving for people with disabilities. I descended to 125 meters (the equivalent of a building 47 stories high or 410 feet) with several tanks and different mixtures of breathing gases. It took me thirteen minutes to get to that depth and more than three hours to return to the surface. I had to give my body time to remove the helium and the nitrogen from my tissues. It was an incredible physical and mental challenge, but it was worth it!

On December 13, 2013, I made my second world-record dive for a person with a disability for distance and time underwater. I dived 15.6 kilometers (nearly 10 miles) over 8:16 hours in the marine park off Cozumel, Mexico. I made the entire dive on a device called a rebreather (the same used by astronauts for space travel) while eating and drinking underwater.

I've made two documentaries. One was *The Story of a Warrior*. It was a biography of me, made around the performance of the first world-record dive. The second was with Jean-Michel Cousteau called *The Current*. It talks about the lives of several people who face personal and physical challenges and how the ocean and scuba diving have changed their lives.

In the 2018, I am preparing my third world-record dive, performing the deepest diving in an underwater cave called the Sabak Ha near Merida, Yucatan. I intend to exceed 130 meters deep. Literally, I will be the deepest disabled diver in the world!

Currently, I am also part of the ranks of Rotary International. That's right, I am an active member of the Rotary Club Cancun Bicentenario, belonging to the District 4195. Rotary allows me to share my experiences with others and work side by side with my peers. It is a great experience. Rotary made me realize how important it is to do for others and work to change lives. I've built really strong relationships and genuine friendships while we work together to help the less fortunate. I fully support the desire to receive only a smile from a child, the elderly, and people with disabilities who have benefited from our efforts. These are all vulnerable groups who need us to help them clear their roads with our experiences. We are the ones who are, in theory, in perfect physical and mental health, and we have a stability that allows us to help them, but we gain more for our lives than they do.

You are young and full of life. You have revolutionary ideas and the skills you need to make a better version of yourself. Think about your life for a moment. What is the meaning of your life? Where are you going? Don't take someone else's life. This beautiful life is yours. It is your history and you are writing it every day, taking every chance. Think about the following:

- Analyze your own skills and your strengths. Write them down. What are your true abilities? What would you like to be?

- What do you consider to be your weaknesses or disabilities? These are areas of opportunity to improve on. You get up late? You do not like school?

- If you don't work at your weaknesses, how can you improve? What would be your plan of action? Set goals for the short, medium and long term and stick to them. Push yourself a little every day.

- Become a leader.

- Make your own decisions.

- Think about what you are passionate about and practice it at least once a week.

- Learn new things: Leave your comfort zone.

Today you'll go home with this story in your mind. My life is full of interesting projects. What about you? You can get up from that chair without any impediment and you can move, run, jump. Will you go home with the same ideas you had in your mind before I started talking? I hope not. Analyze your own capabilities and decide to surpass your own borders and improve your own life. Doing that—being forced to do that—has allowed me to continue my personal growth.

Thank you so much for sharing this time with me, and I can only invite you to dare . . . dare to take the book of your life and enrich it. Write the best stories in it. There is always the opportunity to make it the best story.

Chapter 10

Through the Rotary Club, Leo became involved with Toastmasters so he could improve his speaking ability and hone his presentational skills. Working on his speech one evening in front of Larena, he included a segment about her and how supportive she was to him. She began to cry.

"She told me she had pushed those things aside, but hearing them brought everything back to her. We cried together, and I told her I was sorry. It wasn't my fault, but it wasn't hers, either. If she hadn't been there, I wouldn't be here."

While Leo is a physically imposing figure, with strong arms and broad shoulders, Larena is petite, though this doesn't mean she is any less imposing.

"She is short, like five feet tall. She is not the biggest lady. I want to dedicate a very special part of this to her love and support. It wasn't easy for her or for me.

Without her, I would be dead. In the very beginning, when I was at the bank, I felt a lot of pain and we went to the doctor. He said I was only going to live six months. I started to prepare for death. I said goodbye. She said, 'You're not going anywhere. You are going to stay here.'"

Larena never gave up on him.

"I didn't know she was struggling. In the surgery room, she told me she would be there when I woke up. I never realized she was struggling with the whole idea. All I saw was her strength."

It was only after Larena heard Leo practicing his speech that she admitted to him when she saw him after his surgery, before he woke up, that she cried, thinking he would never be able to handle the loss of his leg.

"When I woke up, all I saw was smiling and energy and confidence."

While Leo realizes his own, obvious disability, he has come to understand what his wife was going through.

"She has a silent disability. We don't always see the support that others give us. We can't do anything without those around us. Nobody told her how to deal with the situation. I can't imagine how demanding it was for her."

Leo said some of his family was not at the hospital during the surgery because he had already told them goodbye. He didn't expect to make it.

"After the surgery, before I woke up, she called everyone. She told them they needed to be strong, not to let me down, and not to show any weakness. She told them they had to be strong for me. We all have bad days.

Imagine having a bad day but still having to put a good face forward. There are a lot of people who don't know how to deal with things like that."

Larena recalls, "I forced myself to do many things and although I always looked very strong and quiet, secretly I cried a lot and prayed to God in secret for his recovery."

Larena has been beside Leo long before the cancer came and will see him through it.

"Since I met him, Leo has always been a charismatic, cheerful, strong, and determined character with great strength to cope. He has always been driven to be different. He is a man of ideas and ideals, a born leader, and the noblest being I've ever met. Regardless of what someone does, he is always ready to forgive and support. Since he was very young, people have always followed him, and he has always been recognized by people around him. He is the sort of person who is always looking to do right.

"Leo has been outgoing since I met him. He enjoyed a lot of parties, alcohol, smoking and anything that represented the world. When he became a bank manager, it became part of his life. He never had a thought or a desire to have a different life, and for more than fourteen years of his life, he missed out on family and the most beautiful but simple things.

"It is undeniable that Leo is now a much better human being than he was before the cancer. These are all God-given gifts, and he wants to use them 100 percent."

Leo and Larena don't have any children, yet. That will change.

"When I was working in the bank, I was feeling like I was the king of the hill. I said, 'We need to wait to have kids.' I wanted to wait until I could give them what they needed. I wanted them to have a better life than I had. When the cancer came, they gave me radiation in my hip. The doctors said it would be impossible to have kids for five years. And then they said I would die before five years."

Now that he has lived beyond his five-year death sentence, Leo is planning for the future.

"I would love for my wife to have kids, to be a mother. I want her to have that blessing. If we can't have our own, we might adopt.

"When preparing for a dive, I discuss everything with my wife. She has a right to know. I am taking risks, but not without her support and understanding of those risks. I know it isn't just my life but our life that hangs in the balance. If she told me it wasn't worth it and the risks were too great, I couldn't do what I do," Leo said.

Larena explained. "When the idea of the world-record dive came up, for me it was very good. Leo always had a passion for high-risk activities. And I always said he preferred to live doing what he wanted and to be happy. The first record was a gift of joy, and although I was a little nervous, I knew that God had given him a second chance to do something big that nobody had done before."

Even after the surgery, Leo struggled without realizing Larena suffered as well.

"The psychiatrists gave me a lot of medication. It slowed down my brain. It wasn't helping me. People who have lost a limb—they think their life is over. My life was not done. I can still love, and I have a great life. There is more to life. It's not the end of life. It's been almost seven years, but we are still learning."

The struggle was real for Larena, too.

"The most difficult part of this process, after he lost his leg, was seeing Leo fall into a deep depression. He wasn't able to be the same person he had always been. He did not want his friends and acquaintances to see him without a leg. Many people think that depression is for months, when, in fact, it can last for years. Leo lost his leg and with it, he lost confidence in himself. He believed deeply in his heart he would die within five years. Pursuing the world records gave him a purpose and something to fight for every day, but he didn't want to make any long-term commitments because he was certain he would not still be alive. That was the hardest part of this process. But thank God we have overcome, and now I see life returning to him in the simplest details and the largest plan. He is beginning to plan for the future."

Chapter 11

On September 18, 2015, Leo was able to give a TED (Technology, Entertainment and Design) talk in Cancun about his efforts to encourage people with disabilities to live to their full potential. TED is a nonprofit organization devoted to spreading ideas in the form of short talks of less than eighteen minutes. The speakers are taught how to distill their ideas and deliver their information in a concise, focused manner.

"Through Facebook, I saw a post announcing the TED conference in Cancun saying, 'If you are interested in giving a TED talk, if you have a story to share, send us your resume to this email address.' Because I worked with disabilities, I thought for sure I had something to say. I sent a short video and biography, along with my motivation for doing this."

The TEDx Cancun organizers replied and said they liked Leo's idea but they had a lot of people who had applied to present. They invited Leo to submit a cell phone video telling them his idea in ninety seconds. He received the e-mail at 11:30 p.m.

"The next morning, I woke up with my wife at six in the morning and told her what I wanted to do. I put on a shirt but was still wearing my pajama pants. I described how I wanted to integrate people with disabilities and make a good example for everyone. We sent the video to the email address."

They later told him he was one of the final contenders and would hear back from them when they made their final decision.

"It was four or five weeks, and I forgot about it. I was moving very quickly on other things. Finally, the email came and said, 'Congratulations, your presentation has been accepted.'"

The TEDx Cancun organizers sent him a schedule for the event. It included training sessions on how to elaborate a story, storytelling, and how to build a presentation. He said the entire process was a great experience, helping him to further hone his message and ability to explain to others what he was trying to do. In all, 150 applied to give talks and 15 speakers were accepted. At the TEDx Cancun event, there were 200 people in the audience.

"I was the only one speaking on behalf of people with disabilities, but I wasn't the only one speaking about the ocean. There were two other divers on the list. One spoke on archeology on human bones in the caves and the cenotes, and the second diver talked about underwater photography to show how we are affecting the ocean in Riviera Maya and Cancun.

"From the fifteen talks, I was the only one who received a standing ovation. Everyone stood and clapped for two or three minutes. It was very touching, but I say I was not speaking about myself. I was speaking about disabilities and the possibilities and the misconceptions of the disabled people."

Leo's profile on the TEDx Cancun website reads:

Leo Morales: Athlete, Disabled Diver, Deep-Diving World Guinness Record, Cancer Survivor

Professional diver and holder of two world records, Leo is a testimony to how to overcome the adversities of life because even after losing his right leg due to a cancerous tumor in the femur, he is training hard to break his own world-record deep dive, reaching 125 meters. Cancun has been for him, the perfect place to begin again, to feed his warrior spirit, and be the bearer of a message of inspiration and strength.

———

In November 2015, Leo attended the DEMA show in Orlando, Florida, where he met with sponsors for his upcoming attempt to break his own world-record deep dive. Returning to Mexico, Leo was shocked to learn his father was in the hospital. His computer had died while he was away so he had not been in contact with his family until he landed at the airport in Cancun.

He got the word that his father was walking down the street and fell. He hit his head. They took him immediately to the hospital.

As soon as he landed in Mexico, Leo went directly to the hospital to join his family and see his father. Leobardo Morales Senior had a stroke and never recovered. He died after eight days in the hospital on November 17, 2015.

"At least I had the chance to say goodbye and to forgive him. I asked him for forgiveness, too. We got the chance to make sure everything was resolved before he died. In the first two days, he was responsive. He could understand, but then after a couple of days, he lost the ability to talk. Finally, his brain died before his body. In the last moment, I presume he was listening. He was connected to the machines and his heart rate and his breathing would change, according to the machines, but he couldn't respond."

Like many fathers and sons, Leo and his father had a complicated relationship. When his parents had divorced, he said it broke his heart completely. After the divorce and his father's return to Mexico City, the elder Leo remarried and had two children with his new wife.

"At the very end, I think he realized the second marriage wasn't what he expected. In the beginning, he told me if something happened to him, I would be responsible for his new children. I agreed, but then after the cancer, I told him it wasn't fair to give me that responsibility. I didn't want to have that responsibility. At the very end, I got very close to him and forgave all of the mistakes."

It was Leo's father that taught him to love the ocean.

"He was crucial for my development. He taught me how to swim. Because of him, I learned to love and respect the ocean. Since I was young, my father was very support-ive of taking me to the ocean. My mother, however, was scared of the ocean. Coming from the Yucatan, she believes the spirits live in the cenotes. She doesn't like that I go into the ocean, but she understands why I do it."

It is possible the older Leo was prescient because he bought Leo his first mask and fins to use at the beach.

"He was always encouraging me to go to ocean and swim. I loved the ocean and the waves and the beach because of him. He always pushed me to go that way. I grew up doing a lot of sports.

"When I lost my leg, I remember my father crying. I asked him why. He said 'I don't know, baby, but I am here for you.' He was giving me a big hug like when I was a child, and it made me feel very protected."

Leo's father bounced back quickly.

"He was very strong, encouraging me and telling me I would get better soon.

"When I found this amazing sport of scuba diving, he was really, really scared. He didn't know what to expect when I was out diving. He had been snorkeling but never under the water. In spite of that, he was very support-ive. He never told me he was scared for me because he wanted to be supportive."

Fortunately for Leo, he realized before his father passed away just how much the man meant to him and how much his father had done for him over the years. Often, people wait too long to say those things to parents and loved ones and miss the chance.

"He was the most amazing father I ever met. Every person has his own limitations, but I started to realize when I got older how much love he had for all of his kids. He made his mistakes, but it is clear how supportive he was for all of us. All fathers make sacrifices for their kids. I can imagine the times he wanted new clothes or a new car and instead he gave us everything he had."

Rest in Peace, Leobardo Morales Santos,
November 17, 2015.

Chapter 12

Since 2008, Leo has felt like he was running all the time. He didn't know if he was running away or running toward something. Likely, it was a little of both. He was running away from his new reality, even though in many ways he adapted to it and molded it into his persona. He was running away from his "death sentence" in the form of the doctor's prediction of how long he would live, assuming he survived the surgery. He was also running toward a new reality. Not Leo without a leg, but Leo the inspiration, the motivator, and the athlete.

"It's been eight years and I look back and say, 'Wow!' I've done a few things and some are positive and some are still hurting me because I haven't faced them.

"The doctors told me that I needed to learn to have a different kind of life. I needed to be cautious. I don't want to stop doing what I'm doing. My youth is not going to be forever. I am still cancer-free, but there will come a day when I can't do what I'm doing. I will have to face it, but I don't want to make any excuses later about not doing what I should be doing to inspire others. I want to always be better. I want to be a better man, a better husband, a better diver and a better person."

Leo is moving forward with plans to make another world-record dive, but at the same time he is learning to appreciate life and not run anymore.

"I think everything happens for a reason. Before this next attempt, my dive accident was a wake-up call. On my next attempt, I am planning to get below 400 feet, but this time also be diving inside a cenote.

"I am being very cautious and don't want to be the kind of person who isn't. I learned my lesson."

He acknowledges that he was in such a rush before because he thought he was running out of time. He tried to do everything at once. Now that he has exceeded his five-year life expectancy, he has a new perspective.

Leo experienced grief in the true, classical sense. While everyone handles grief differently, and moves through the stages on their own terms, they are generally acknowledged as shock or disbelief, denial, bargaining, guilt, anger, depression, and acceptance/hope.

Stan Patterson of POA said, "Because there are so few hip disarticulates and only a small percentage of them utilize prostheses, it is important for those who do to show what is possible. Leo told us that in Mexico many people with disabilities are deemed inferior and unable to work—shunned by the community. He is determined to do his best to change that perception by example.

"An amputee will go through stages of grief as they mourn the loss of their limb. To what degree will depend on personality and circumstances of the individual. What has been helpful to patients in our practice is peer support—meeting other amputees who understand what they are feeling and can demonstrate life goes on and is still good. While he was still healing and receiving treatment for cancer, Leo scoured the Internet for information and was inspired by what he saw was possible. The more he learned, the less scared and more optimistic he was. In Leo's case, he was fortunate enough to have the means available for him to travel and tour some of the best prosthetic facilities in the world. That is not an option for most people, but researching them via the Internet is."

Receiving the prosthetic leg from Stan Patterson and POA was a gift for Leo. It helped him see the possibilities of life and get him moving forward. Unfortunately, the device has now exceeded its mechanical life expectancy and he can't afford to have it updated.

"I don't have any health insurance and I don't have the money to have the device fixed. Just the knee alone will cost $20,000. I had to make the decision of continuing diving or fixing my leg. I chose scuba."

Leo realized he needed to accept himself as he is. That took him time, but he is comfortable with the decision.

"Every penny I have I invest in diving because I know that is where I can do the most good for people with disabilities. I don't have enough money to do everything I want to do, but I am doing the best I can."

Leo's wife Larena is a school principal now and Leo teaches diving classes and works as a dive guide. He has sponsors for his dives, supplying him with equipment, but none of them pay him a salary.

"It has been really tough being a disabled athlete, but I have a lot of faith I am doing what I am supposed to be doing. All of my energy is focused on this. It demands a lot of time, energy and money. Sometimes I think I have to quit and go back to the real world."

Finding a real job would certainly make life easier for Leo, but he says he still believes in what he is doing.

"Any time I hear from someone that I have inspired them or helped them, it helps, but it is still a struggle."

Leo knows how fortunate he is now.

"I've been having a great life so far. I've been happier in the last seven years than in my life before that. I am a complete man. I am very grateful for the life I have. I am all about tasting life and enjoying my family. I'm not about chasing money anymore. I'm not a greedy guy. I'm not about counting pennies."

He concedes the process hasn't been easy for him, but he welcomes the opportunities losing his leg to cancer have given him.

"I was angry before, but now I am very grateful for the people who are showing up in my life. I consider myself one of the luckiest people in the world. I'm not rich, but rich in friends."

Since learning to dive and realizing how he could use his own personal situation to inspire others, with and without disabilities, Leo has changed personally and professionally. There are some who imagine he is making the dives for personal gain or for fame. The only way to silence the critics is to prove them wrong.

"I still hope to open a facility that helps disabled people. In Mexico, we don't have the culture of taking care of others with disabilities. I want to change that."

He knows it will take a lot of work and perseverance. "I will never quit. I am struggling with the bureaucracy and the empty promises. Sometimes I get frustrated and am tempted to give up. But then I think about the times in the hospital when I didn't give up. I'm not going to give up now. I want to bring together more people who have the same ideals to work together for people with disabilities. There are so many things I want to change about the way we are here in Mexico, but it is really frustrating to hit the wall every time. In spite of that, great things are happening. There are no limitations when you have a dream. We are not disabled people."

Leo has begun CrossFit, which is a great example of his desire to move forward and prepare for the challenges ahead. CrossFit is a cross-training exercise system that is a challenge itself.

"In order to drop some weight and improve my flexibility, I'm doing CrossFit. It is very demanding. They force you to move all of your body, especially for an old dude like me. The trainers do yoga as well. We do that after a demanding workout. I am going to start practicing these breathing exercises for this deep dive. It is pranayama, like freedivers use when they begin a dive. They slow down their heartbeat and breathe to focus on the dive. The guys have been very supportive with my leg. I am sure I am not the only guy who is doing Cross-Fit without a limb. We are adapting exercises. We move it to the floor but keep my heart rate very high. At my age, I am still exploring stuff."

Leo keeps moving forward and never gives up.

Chapter 13

Leo's next dive will be to surpass his own first world record by going even deeper, but this time there will be an additional challenge. His third world-record dive will be to attempt 150 meters (500 feet) underwater inside a cenote.

For the ancient Mayans living in the region of the Yucatan and Quintana Roo, cenotes were openings to the underworld. They knew the cool freshwater inside was good for swimming and cooling off from the heat, but they also believed the cenotes were a direct connection to their gods. They offered sacrifices into them and prayed in front of them.

Often, these cenotes are hundreds of feet deep and then spread out farther, as they lead inside their tunnels and caves.

Leo's plan for his third world-record dive is to dive inside the cenote Sabak Ha in the Yucatan. It is approximately thirty miles away from the city of Merida, where his mother is from. Sabak Ha means dark waters in Mayan. The bottom is so deep that no one in the ancient world knew how deep it went. They thought it led directly to Xibalba or Metnal, both names for the hell of the Mayan world. Xibalba was a fearsome place and the only way to escape it was to die a violent death.

Leo plans to descend into Sabak Ha and then return to the surface. He is excited about being able to make this third world-record attempt in the Yucatan, near where he grew up and learned to appreciate nature.

The state of Yucatan has 2,560 cenotes. He hopes to draw attention to the natural richness and encourage ecotourism and adventure tourism in the region by taking advantage of the media he attracted with his first two dives. This media included:

- Televisa
- TV Azteca
- Telemundo
- Fox Sports
- TDN
- ESPN

He also received remarkable coverage in newspapers, magazines, and social media. It is estimated that his first two dives touched more than 200 million people worldwide.

Leo's first two world-record dives were completed on a shoestring budget with friends and volunteers. As he has achieved more notoriety and gained more attention, he now understands the need for more elaborate preparations. And with that comes greater expense.

"With the first two events, we did it with our own money. We didn't know how much it would take to do it, but we did it anyway. I really enjoyed it," he said. "With this dive, I am trying to be more organized and get more support. I don't want to get paid for doing the dive. I'm not in this to make money. I want to inspire and promote the region. For the next dive, ideally, I would like to touch 130 meters (500 feet), but at least I will go below my previous record. I want the dive to be certified by Guinness World Records. I want to do something different and want to raise money for disabled people or cancer patients. I want every meter to make sense and help someone—120 meters to help 120 disabled people with wheelchairs or diving training. Something like that. I want to develop something that really helps."

When Leo began his quest to set world records and draw attention to the disability community in Mexico and around the world, he became the first athlete sponsored by Cressi Mexico.

"I don't think they realized what I had planned. Cressi had given me everything I asked for, but they are a recreational diving company. They don't have technical gear."

Leo has had to look for other sponsors when his equipment needs have surpassed what Cressi is able to provide to him, like the Nautilus rebreathers he used on the second world-record dive.

"DEMA 2015 was a great platform for me. We made contacts with the people we needed. I needed a dry suit and we found a sponsor, as well as an underwater lighting sponsor," he explained.

While the water inside Mexican cenotes is warm, often in the mid 700F range, when you are exposed to it for hours during both the exploration and decompression phase, a dry suit that offers greater thermal protection is a must. Also, in contrast to the world-record dives in the open ocean, there is no sunlight deep inside a cenote, so additional lighting equipment is mandatory.

For this dive, Leo returns to the world of open-circuit diving, venting the exhaled breathing gases to the water around him. He plans to use a mixture of breathing gases specially blended for the dive using helium, oxygen, and nitrogen. He has planned a series of training dives both in shallow water and at depth to practice the skills and techniques necessary to complete a complex dive of this nature. He will practice a series of drills to give him the technical and psychological ability to deal with problems that might arise while underwater.

Leo's near-miss dive brought home the lesson he must drill and prepare for every possible scenario. To make the dive, he must be completely comfortable with handling multiple scuba cylinders with various gas mixtures for various depths and distinguish between the appropriate regulators for each. He has to know where each cylinder and the gas supply valves are located on his body and how they are attached to his equipment in case he needs to close one off and open a secondary valve in an emergency. With all of the additional scuba cylinders attached to his body, he also has to practice swimming with the gear configurations to make sure he is properly adjusted in the water and comfortable.

Other concerns include:

- Emergency management

- Gas management

- Team protocols

- Underwater communications

- Dive and decompression planning

- Breathing gas analysis

- First aid and dive accident management

To practice and drill for this world-record attempt, Leo plans at least ten work-up dives. They include:

1. 21/79 air dive to 66 meters

2. 16/24 trimix dive to 72 meters

3. 16/24 trimix dive to 72 meters

4. 14/33 trimix dive to 85 meters

5. 14/33 trimix dive to 85 meters

6. 12/40 trimix dive to 100 meters

7. 12/40 trimix dive to 100 meters

8. 8/50 trimix dive to 100 meters

9. 8/50 trimix dive to 100 meters

10. 6/70 trimix dive to 120 meters

Each of those numbers represents a dive and the particular gas mix necessary to make it safely. The first number is the oxygen content in the breathing gas Leo will breathe at depth. The second number represents the percentage of helium in the breathing gas. The remainder of the gas is made up with nitrogen. Helium is used to reduce the amount of nitrogen that can build up in the divers' tissues and lower the amount of oxygen in the breathing gas. At depth, oxygen can become toxic to the diver, so Leo will have to breathe reduced levels.

Each dive will be supported by a team of divers and support personnel with training in dive accident management along with first aid and oxygen delivery. A hyperbaric chamber set up to treat injured divers will remain on alert to be used in case of an accident. When divers are injured in a dive accident or exhibit signs of decompression sickness (the bends), they are placed inside a hyperbaric chamber and the chamber is pressurized. Typically, the divers are returned to a pressure equal to that found at 18 meters (60 feet) of seawater. From there, they return to surface pressure slowly while breathing oxygen to help remove the accumulated excess nitrogen from their bodies.

It takes a well-trained and skilled team to complete a dive of this magnitude. This dive will include divers who have been with Leo for the first two dives and others experienced in ultra-deep diving technique.

This dive will also come with official recognition. The Mexican Federation of Underwater Activities, (an active member of the International Olympic Committee), Sports Confederation Mexican, and Mexican Olympic Committee will be on hand to certify the dive. Also, the World Underwater Federation, founded by Jacques Cousteau will be there to endorse the record. Lastly, Leo plans to have representatives from the Guinness World Records on hand to certify the dive.

Chapter 14

I asked Dr. Dario Gomez what makes Leo so special.

"When you meet him, he has the ability to connect with people. He calls you brother or *hermano* and becomes a true friend. You listen to his story and learn about his fight and how he got to the place he is now. I believe it is very difficult not to feel inspired after listening to him."

I asked the same question of Stan Patterson at Prosthetic and Orthotic Associates. His response was similar.

"Leo is an awesome guy! He has inspired countless people with his positive energy, can-do spirit, and amazing successes. And what makes him even more special is his dedication toward paying it forward and helping other amputees, especially hip disarticulates, believe in themselves and experience success. Leo is the real deal! He has tremendous belief in himself and that all things are possible if you try hard enough. Leo has never wavered in his determination to live a full and active life and educate the world by his example, 'The only disability is in the mind.' He even learned how to run with a running blade, something no other hip disarticulate (at that time) had been successful at." (A prosthetic running blade is a specially designed foot prosthetic that gives the runner extra spring with each step.)

Larena, the person who knows Leo better than anyone, including Leo, summed it up this way.

"I have accompanied Leo for twenty-three years, and I am sure the feeling of admiration and respect I feel for him now is the most intense. I love him for his perseverance and passion in everything he does. When he has an idea, he does not stop until he reaches it.

"It is important for Leo to continue sending a message about the capabilities of the disabled and choosing life over death. Leo is a survivor of a very rare and aggressive type of cancer. It's a miracle he's alive. In the process of saving his life, Leo had to go through one of the hardest struggles, losing his foot, knee, and all the way to his hip. The highest percentage of these amputees do not return to everyday life. Leo is an inspiration and example of how to achieve a normal life, from driving to going to a buffet to fill his dish and bring it to the table.

"For me, it is very important that Leo is changing the culture in Mexico by showing that he is a whole man despite not having a leg. Through various activities such as lectures, talks, sporting events, and diving, his message of being the best version of ourselves continues spreading. Every day he is working to support people with disabilities."

If the story ended there, it would be enough. Everything taken away from him, Leo rose like a phoenix from the ashes that he spoke of in his Rotary speech to find a new purpose in life. He had overcome the challenges life threw at him and still moved forward. In the ocean, Leo has found a place where he was no longer disabled. A brief timeline of Leo's accomplishments are listed in Appendix C: Accomplishments and Presentations. But that's not the end. The story is just beginning. The play that is Leobardo Morales Cervantes has just started the Second Act.

While Leo will tell you diving saved his life, the next thing he will tell you is his mission in life is to inspire others. He has dedicated his life to working to support others who have disabilities, making sure they are treated fairly. More importantly, he is working to make adaptive scuba diving available in Mexico through the foundation A Mar Abierto AC. The name has a dual translation of both Open Sea and Open Heart.

I am confident we haven't heard the last of Leo and his efforts. He will keep greeting people, making new friends, and challenging everyone he meets to do better and push to improve themselves.

As Leo says, "Nothing is impossible!"

He truly is dive-abled.

Appendix A

Dive Team for December 5, 2012 World-Record Dive

German Yañez, Main Coordinator

Cesar Zepeda, Main coordinator for Staff
and Sponsor of the Boat

Mario Chavez, Videographer and Cameraman

Luz Maria Guzman, Support Diver

Jorge Camarena, Support Diver

Geraldine Solignac, Support Diver

Oliver Prats, Support Diver

Raymundo Rivera, Support Diver

Alejandra Jimenez, Support Diver

Robert Belanger, Support Diver

Carlos Cardiel, Support Diver

Francisco Kyle, Photographer

Michael D Viau, Photographer

Monica Aguilar, Filmmaker

Marco Bortignon, Photographer

Dr. J. Dario Gomez C, Medical Director of
Costamed Hyperbaric
Chamber

Buzos del Caribe, Diving Operation

El Esfuerzo, Boat

Captain "Huacho" and Sailor "Chavelo"

Appendix B

Dive Crew for 2013 World-Record Dive

German Yañez

Cesar Zepeda

Robert Belanger

Alejandra Jimenez

Dr. J. Dario Gomez C, the Medical Director of Costamed Hyperbaric Chambers

Dr. Mathias Nochetto, Latin America Medical Director

Roberto Perez, Surface Coordinator.

Casey Omholt, Nautilus Rebreather Sponsor

Buzos del Caribe, Diving Operation

El Esfuerzo, Boat

Captain "Huacho" and Sailor "Chavelo"

Appendix C

Accomplishments and Presentations

2012

- December 4, 2012: Achieved depth world record for people with disabilities 125 meters (412 feet deep), Cozumel, Mexico.

- December 2012: Documentary *Leo Morales: A Warrior's Story* filmed.

2013

- March 10: Press conference in Cancun announced the second world-record dive.

- April: Documentary *The Current* with Jean-Michel Cousteau filmed.

- September 10: Completed the diving instructor course in the Heroic Naval Academy in Veracruz to become the only diver with disabilities to graduate from the Mexican Navy.

- October 8: Completed PADI Instructor Development Course in Playa del Carmen. (One of the few PADI dive instructors with disabilities in the world.)

- November 24: Became an instructor for the Handicap Scuba Association in Denver,

Colorado, to teach diving to people with disabilities.

- November 30: Presentation of the documentary *Leo Morales: A Warrior's Story* in Calpe, Spain. He was named Knight Diver for bringing together diving and disabilities.

- Documentary *Leo Morales: A Warrior's Story* released in Mexico in December 2013.

- December 13: Achieved time and distance world record for persons with disabilities. Dived 8 hours 16 minutes and covered 15,600 meters (10 Miles) near Cozumel.

2014

- February 14: *The Current* premiered in Denver, Colorado.

- September 16: Traveled to Dahab, Egypt, as a judge at the world deep-diving record by Ahmed Gabr. (Gabr is currently the deepest diver in the world, reaching 335 meters [1,100 feet] deep.)

- September 26: Dived the Blue Hole in Dahab, Egypt, to 63 meters (205 feet) deep and became the first disabled person to dive it.

- October 12: Attended the national premiere of *The Current* in Mexico City at the World Trade Center and closure of the Expo Buceo.

- November 20: *The Current* shown at DEMA, Las Vegas, Nevada.

- December 10: *The Current* shown at the Cozumel Scuba Fest.

2015

- January 28: Participated in the inauguration of the park for people with disabilities in Playa del Carmen. The park was named for Leo and his work to change the perception of people with disabilities.

- Feb 17: Became an instructor for Ocean Reef's Full Face Mask.

- May 15: Presented to 350 Young Rotarians for the Rotary Club International, Cancun, Mexico.

- June 06: Was the guest of honor during an attempt to set a new Guinness World Record in Hurghada, Egypt, to have the most divers in the water at one time (650) with world-record deep diver Ahmed Gabr.

- June 16: Became a rotarian.

- September 18: Presented "The Best Version of Yourself" at TEDx Conference, Cancun, Mexico.

- October 9: Traveled to Mexico City to be part of "Expo Buceo Mexico" as a member of the Cressi Mexico Team.

- November 03: Traveled to Orlando, Florida, to participate in DEMA SHOW 2015.

- December 07: Became a PADI freediving instructor in Quintana Roo, Mexico.

Acknowledgments

I infinitely thank my dear friend Eric Douglas, who has given me his time and passion as a writer to share this story.

I express my heartfelt gratitude to all who are always willing to help, to those who change the world with their small actions, and to those who give hope to people about to surrender in life.

Finally, I do not want to stop thanking all the people who are fighting cancer or who suffer a disability of any kind. You are my inspiration. Remember: attitude and faith are the key to achieve all your dreams.

Leo Morales

About the Authors

ERIC DOUGLAS

Photo courtesy of Daniel Boyd

Life is an adventure for Eric Douglas, above and below the water and wherever in the world he ends up. Eric received a degree in journalism from Marshall University. After working in local newspapers, honing his skills as a storyteller and following a stint as a freelance journalist in the former Soviet Union, he became a dive instructor. The ocean and diving have factored into all of his fiction works since then.

Eric is the former Assistant Editor of PADI's *The Undersea Journal*, the former Director of Training for Divers Alert Network, and is currently the Lessons for Life columnist for *Scuba Diving Magazine*. He co-authored the book *Scuba Diving Safety* with Dan Orr.

As a documentarian and biographer, Eric has worked in Russia, Honduras, and most recently in his home state of West Virginia, featuring the oral histories of West Virginia war veterans in the documentary *West Virginia Voices of War* and the companion book *Common Valor*.

His book *Keep On, Keepin' On* is a biography of Jean Hanna Davis as she went through chemotherapy for breast cancer for the second time in ten years.

Eric talks about adventure, taking time to be creative, diving, and writing on his blog on his website at www. booksbyeric.com. You can follow him on Twitter, get in touch on Facebook or Google+, or send him an e-mail at eric@booksbyeric.com.

BOOKS BY ERIC DOUGLAS

River Town

Withrow Key Short Stories
*Tales from Withrow Key:
A Collection of
Thriller Short Stories*

Going Down with the Ship

Bait and Switch

Put It Back

Frog Head Key

Queen Conch

Sea Monster

Caesar's Gold

Life Under the Sea

Lyin' Fish

Children's Books
*The Sea Turtle Rescue
and Other Stories*

Mike Scott Adventures
Cayman Cowboys

Flooding Hollywood

Guardians' Keep

Wreck of the Huron

Heart of the Maya

*Return to Cayman:
Paradise Held Hostage*

Oil and Water

*The 3rd Key:
Sharks in the Water*

Nonfiction
*Heart Survivor:
Recovery After Heart Surgery*

*Capturing Memories:
Recording Oral Histories*

*Keep on, Keepin' on:
A Breast Cancer Survivor Story*

Common Valor

Russia: The New Age

Scuba Diving Safety

Photo courtesy of Brandon P. Watts

LEO MORALES

Leo Morales is a disabled diver and an international English-Spanish motivational speaker. Currently, he is preparing for a third world record for scuba diving in a cenote in Quintana Roo. He is an ambassador of the international diving brands PADI, Cressi, XDeep, Intova.

In 2016 *Sports Illustrated* included Leo in a list of people in sports with disabilities. Through his foundation, Open Sea, he promotes diving for people with disabilities.

www.ingramcontent.com/pod-product-compliance
Lightning Source LLC
Chambersburg PA
CBHW072022040426
42447CB00009B/1696